MS-DOS

3.3 to 5.0

CW00322412

Peter Freese

MS-DOS
3.3 to 5.0

PRISMA
COMPUTER
COURSE

Prisma Computer Courses first published in Great Britain 1992 by

McCarta Ltd
15 Highbury Place
London N5 1QP

Translation: George Hall
Production: LINE UP text productions

© Rowohlt Taschenbuch Verlag GmbH, Reinbek bei Hamburg
For the English translation
© 1992 Uitgeverij Het Spectrum B.V., Utrecht

ISBN 1 85365 330 6

British Library Cataloguing-in-Publication Data.
A catalogue record for this book is available from the British Library.

Contents

Foreword

The MS-DOS operating system has become the standard operating system for personal computers since the
largest computer manufacturer, IBM, adopted this system for its products. Many other computer manufacturers have also adopted this system. This has led to an
even more rapid expansion of this operating system.

For most computer users, the choice of a certain operating system depends upon whether good and inexpens-
ive application programs can be run under this system.
MS-DOS can certainly satisfy this criterion. Thousands
of programs are based upon this system.

This book provides a clear introduction to working with
personal computers which make use of the MS-DOS
operating system. Equipped with this know-how, you
will be able to work with most MS-DOS computers such
as:

■ The PC (Personal Computer), the computer with the
  Intel 8088/8086 processor and one or two diskdrives.
■ The XT computer (eXtended Technology), a PC with
  a harddisk.
■ The AT computer (Advanced Technology), a PC with
  the fast 80286 or 80386 processor, mostly with one
  diskdrive and a harddisk.

This book is meant to be a supplement to the manuals
supplied along with the computer. Computer manuals
do not make pleasant reading in general, due to the fact
that they describe not only the important but also the
unimportant details. In addition, the choice of language
in a manual is often incomprehensible to the beginner.
For these reasons, this book restricts itself to the information necessary to work with the computer in practice.
This book deals with all DOS versions up to, and including, DOS 5.

The text is aided by diagrams and practical exercises.
All the exercises have been developed on an IBM PC
and have been tested on a compatible Nixdorf computer.

Foreword

1 First steps

The most important components and accessories of the personal computer are:

- the system unit with one or two diskdrives; there may also be a harddisk
- the keyboard
- the monitor (the screen)
- the printer.

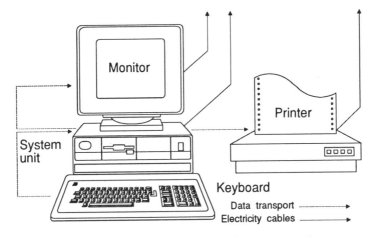

Monitor

Printer

System unit

Keyboard

Data transport ----------→
Electricity cables ----------→

The letters MS, in the name MS-DOS, are an abbreviation of the name of the manufacturer, Microsoft. The letters DOS represent 'disk operating system'. The magnetic storage disk may be a harddisk, which is also called a fixed disk, or a floppy disk (diskette).

Components of a computer: an outline of the workings

In order to understand the task of the operating system, we shall describe the most important computer components, categorized according to function.

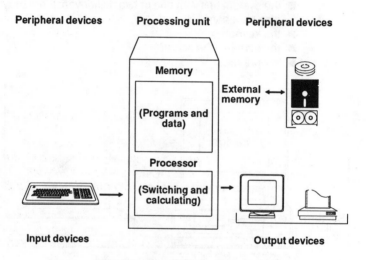

A complete computer, a device for electronic data processing (EDP), consists of two groups of components:

■ the central processing unit (CPU)
■ the peripheral devices.

The central processing unit consists mainly of:

■ one or more processors
■ the memory.
Important peripheral devices are:

■ input: keyboard, mouse, scanner etc
■ output: screen, printer, loudspeaker etc
■ external memory: magnetic disk, optic disk (CD ROM), magnetic tape etc.

The tangible EDP system devices are called *hardware*. Programs are called *software*. (In the extended meaning, lists and collections of data also fall into the category 'software'.)

An operating system must execute the following duties:

- managing and controlling the execution of a program
- managing the input and output of information
- managing files on external media
- managing peripheral devices
- implementing your instructions
- registering errors in the devices and in the operation of these
- saving, adjusting and stating date and time when required
- making conversion and test programs accessible
- (sometimes) managing simultaneous usage of the computer from different work points in a network
- (sometimes) implementing different programs simultaneously (multitasking)
- activating utility programs to safeguard information.

These duties are carried out by routines at two different levels:

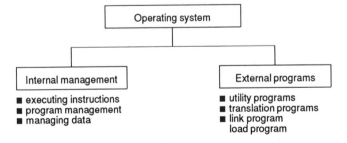

Check before switching on the computer. Most components receive electricity by means of their own electricity cable (though often the system unit has a socket for the monitor). In addition, the peripheral devices must be connected to the system unit for the transport of data.

Check if all cables are in order before switching on the computer. The plugs of the cables used for data transport (interface cables) often have small screws or clips to prevent them becoming loose. Make sure these are well-connected. The cable usage is not identical for all sorts and types. Consult the instruction book.

Most personal computer configurations contain the following cables and connections:

The system unit, the monitor (screen) and the printer have their own (detachable) *electricity cable*. (An earthed plug is preferable.)

The monitor, the printer and the keyboard are connected to the system unit by *interface cables*.

Most *printers* are connected to the parallel interface of the system unit. The following text often occurs next to the connector:

PRINTER
PARALLEL PORT
CENTRONICS (name of the standard parallel interface)
PRINTER PORT

The connection for the *monitor* depends on the way the display component of the system unit has been equipped. There are display adapters for monochrome monitors (green, amber, white) and for colour screens. Occasionally, the system unit has more than one connection. The most common names are:

MONITOR
MONOCHROME MONITOR
COLOUR MONITOR
VIDEO, TV
RGB (red, green, blue)

The *keyboard* connection seldom causes mis-understanding:

KEYBOARD, KEYB

Finally, check if there are still pieces of cardboard in the diskdrive slots. These pieces of cardboard are identical in size to the floppies. They protect the moving parts of the drives against damage during transport.

Groups of keys. Four groups of keys with different functions are located on the keyboard:

■ typewriter keys
■ numerical keys
■ operation keys
■ special keys and function keys.

The typewriter keys. The numbers and letters in the typewriter keypad work in exactly the same way as on a normal typewriter. The Shift keys change a letter to a capital letter, or to the upper character if two characters are shown on the key. In order to type a number of capitals successively, you can switch to the upper case by pressing CapsLock - this mode has no effect on the special characters on the number keys or on the punctuation marks. A small lamp will light up when the capital letter mode is active. In this mode, you can produce small letters by holding down Shift.
The hard carriage return on a typewriter (begin new line) is represented on a computer by the Enter key (may also read 'Return' and /or show an arrow pointing leftwards with short vertical extension).

The numeric keypad. The numeric keypad at the right-hand side of the keyboard facilitates the typing of numbers because you can type them with one hand. Normally these keys have the function of moving the cursor on the screen. Only when the numeric mode has been switched on using the NumLock key, will these keys generate numbers. There is also a small light to indicate this mode. Press NumLock again to switch back to the normal mode.

The following keys in the numeric keypad have functions in text editing:

■ on the 2, 4, 6 and 8 keys, there are arrows for relocating the cursor. Under MS-DOS, only the leftwards arrow (delete) and the rightwards (move) have effect. The Backspace key in the typewriter block can also be used to delete characters to the left.
■ on the 0 key, there is also Ins (insert). This function produces an empty position in the text in order to insert a character. This also applies to the text of the previous instruction in the input buffer of MS-DOS (see chapter 2).
■ on the decimal point key, there is also Del (delete). This function deletes the character at the current position. Under MS-DOS, you delete characters to the right in the input buffer.

The remaining number keys in this pad produce no effect under MS-DOS. Their further functions depend upon the application. In a word-processor, that is mostly as follows:

Home	(7)	cursor to beginning of the line
End	(1)	cursor to end of the line
PgUp	(9)	move to the previous (screen) page
PgDn	(3)	move to the next (screen) page

On MF keyboards, between the typewriter pad and the numeric keypad, there is a set of keys with positioning functions similar to those in the numeric keypad. The advantage of these is that they are logically grouped and that they remain available when working in the numeric mode.

Operation keys. Adjacent to the numeric keypad on PC keyboards, there are two keys with the names:

Scroll Lock/Break	stop screen contents (output) rolling

Print Screen (PrtSc)   transport screen contents to
                           the printer

On an MF keyboard these functions are divided over
three keys:

Print Screen   print screen contents
Scroll Lock   has no function under
                           MS-DOS
Pause   interrupt command
                           (for example, scroll)

In the upper left-hand corner and along the bottom, you
will find the following operation keys:

Esc   return to the previous activity
Ctrl   control, regulate
Alt   alternate, another code

On MF keyboards there are two Ctrl and Alt keys. In
some applications it does make a difference whether
you use the right or the left key. This also applies to
Shift. We refer you to chapter 2 for an outline of the
operation keys under MS-DOS.

In applications, these keys mostly acquire another
meaning:

Esc   quit the main program or the
                           current module
Alt+other key(s)   generate another character
Ctrl+other key(s)   execute an operating
                           instruction

Function keys. There are two vertical rows of five function keys on the PC keyboard. On an MF keyboard,
there is a row of twelve function keys at the top. Their
function depends to a large extent on the application
(often the help menu is activated by F1). There are few
programs which use F11 and F12.
Under MS-DOS, only the keys F1 to F6 have a function
when entering instructions (see chapter 2).

Note: In principle you may redefine each key, allocating it a different effect, but in order to do this, the ANSI.SYS keyboard/screen driver has to be adjusted. (ANSI: American National Standards Institute.) To do this, you really require a thorough knowledge of programming using ASSEMBLER, but nowadays, you can also purchase utilities which can assume this task. It is also possible to define a key otherwise, using an ANSI command (escape sequence). However, it lies outside the scope of this book to deal with this topic more extensively.

Section 9.3 gives a little more information concerning types of keyboard.

Disk memory

A personal computer can only work if the disk containing the system programs is available. In addition, it is generally necessary to permanently (externally) save the programs or the information which you produce or calculate. If you do not do this, this data will be lost as soon as you switch the computer off. A harddisk has the advantage over a diskette in that it works at a greater speed and has a much larger capacity.

The price of harddisks has decreased to the extent that almost all personal computers are now equipped with them. PCs with only one diskdrive are beginning to become a rarity.

The great advantage of diskettes is that they can easily be transported and that they provide cheap and flexible storage of backups of programs and information. For this reason, we shall we shall pay special attention to diskette management in this section. More information concerning types of diskette can be found in section 9.4.

Disk management under MS-DOS

MS-DOS manages disks using a letter, beginning with A. The first harddisk is always C, even if there is only one diskdrive. The position and relative situation of the disk-drives in the system unit differs according to type. This may have tedious consequences if you save files on the wrong diskette when using an unfamiliar computer.

You can allocate another letter to a drive by using the ASSIGN command. In order to activate a program or to load a data file, you generally have to specify the letter of the source drive in the instruction. However, this is not necessary if the source drive is the current drive (i.e. the drive whose letter is shown in the system prompt on the screen. Instead of 'A>DIR A:' you can simply type 'A>DIR'.

Saving programs and data

The contents of a program or a collection of data is writ-ten to a diskette as a *file* with its own name. The infor-mation concerning files (name, size, position, attributes, date etc) is registered in a separate part of the diskette. The contents of the file are written in the data section of the diskette in binary form.

The contents of a file are not directly legible. Only an application program, which has been activated in mem-ory, is able to load, interpret and display a file.
If a file on a diskette is an executable file (program file), it can only become active when it has been loaded in memory by an instruction and then started up (see chapter 1).

New diskettes are not yet ready to receive information - there are no markings allowing the information to be re-trieved. The preparation of a diskette is called *format-ting*. MS-DOS has a program called FORMAT which carries out this operation. This program makes circular magnetic tracks on which the information is written in miniscule magnetic patterns. Each track is divided into sectors - the quantity differs according to type of diskette.

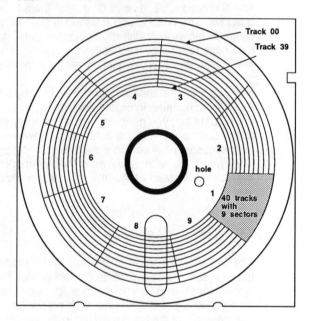

The treatment of diskettes

When using diskettes, nothing can go wrong as long as you treat them with care. The 5.25 inch diskettes, in particular, are vulnerable to pressure, bending, dirt, high or low temperatures and magnetic fields. The diskettes mostly bite the dust only after a reasonable length of time unless they have been badly treated. 3.5 inch diskettes are less sensitive to mechanical maltreatment due to the sturdy plastic casing and the sleeve over the opening for the write/read head. This is, however, no reason to carry them loosely in a jacket pocket full of breadcrumbs.

The following good habits also apply to advanced users!

■ Make a backup of important information and programs.
■ Place a diskette in a paper holder directly after use.
■ Do not touch the write surface.
■ Write the label while it is still on the sticker sheet. Do not erase on the diskette.
■ Keep and transport diskettes in a plastic or hard cardboard box.
■ Do not allow diskettes to be influenced by extremely high or low temperatures. Be wary of dust and cigarette ash. Keep the diskettes away from strong magnetic fields (telephone, electromotors, electromagnets).

Files and file names

A collection of information can only be saved in the form of a file. The operating system finds a file by its name. You may choose the name freely, but it must conform to these rules:

■ A *file name* consists of a maximum of *eight* alphanumeric characters or other allowed characters. For example:
TABLE
TEXT13
PROTOCOL

■ A file name may have an extension consisting of a point and a maximum of *three* characters. For example:
FILENAME.DAT
HOUSE.111
12345678.XYZ

■ Internally, MS-DOS fills up short names and short or missing extensions with spaces. You have already seen in the file lists that the point of the extension is not shown. For example:

LETTER.TXT   LETTER____ TXT
INTER86.3   INTER86_ 3__
NOW   NOW_____ ___

■ You may write file names using small or capital letters. Internally, MS-DOS uses only capitals. For
example:
saving86.xyz   SAVING86 XYZ
OldFile.ABC   OLDFILE ABC

■ A file name may only occur once on the same dis-
kette (unless in different directories). The same file
name may, of course, occur on different diskettes.
Files may have the same name if the extension dif-
fers. For example:
NOTES.001
NOTES.002
NOTES.003

In versions prior to 3.0, file names may not contain characters with accents (ASCII codes above 127). This is
permitted in more recent versions (for instance, using
Alt+number), but this is not applicable to all characters.
For this reason, you should only use normal letters and,
of the special characters, only the hyphen or the underlining.

Due to the fact that some characters have an operating
function under MS-DOS, they may not be included in
file names.

**The following characters are not valid in file or di-
rectory names:**

. , ; : = + < > [ ] / \ | * ?

**A name may not include spaces, even at the begin-
ning.**

■ Under MS-DOS, some names are reserved for special files, names of devices, temporary files and utility
files. If you use these names for your own files, there

is a risk that MS-DOS will interpret them according to their own reserved meaning. At worst, the information will be lost.

Obvious file names

Always give a file a meaningful name, so that you (roughly) know what the contents are without having to have them displayed. The standard extensions which applications and translation programs (compiler, interpreter, assembler) assign, assist you in this.

Examples of meaningful names:

ADDRESS.BAS   = BASIC program which deals
                       with adresses
MEMBERS.ADD   = members address file
GASMETER.Y92   = gas meter figures 1992
AGENDA.TXT   = heading of meeting agenda
UGHH4392.TXT   = inlaws coming to dinner 4th
                       of March 1992
MMMM4992.123   = plans for evening out with
                       new boy/girlfriend

AT computers

Before you can begin using an AT computer, it is necessary to install and register the hardware components using a special start-up program. Fortunately, this is generally done by the manufacturer or the supplier. We shall not discuss here what the program demands and performs, we shall only make a couple of remarks.

Actually installing the hardware. An AT configuration can consist of several components, for example, two diskdrives, two harddisks, various serial and parallel interfaces, a video card for a monochrome or colour screen, memory with capacity between 512 Kb and 16 Mb. Without special measures, MS-DOS is only able to address 640 Kb memory directly. For all components, you must consult the manuals and other documentation.

Configuring the hardware. The computer components can only work when they are aware of each other's existence. They must be registered using a utility. This utility is mostly located on the system diskette under the name SETUP, or it is stored in a small memory which saves the information with the assistence of a battery (CMOS memory), or in the ROM BIOS.

Activate the utility on the diskette using the SETUP instruction, or directly from the permanent memory using the key combination Alt+Ctrl+Esc. If the program is not present in your system, you must acquire it.

The SETUP utility procedure differs according to type, but the program on the Advanced AT Diagnostic Disk from IBM has functioned as an example in most cases. It implements the following tasks (among others):

- checks the system
- registers the system components
- physically formats the harddisk.

Switching on the computer and starting up the operating system

Loading the operating system from a system disk
1 Ensure that the diskdrive locks are open.

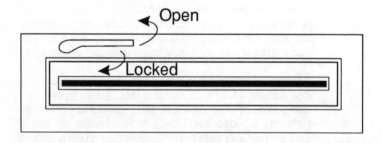

2 Turn on the system unit switch. Often the monitor has its own electricity supply.

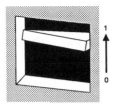

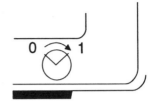

**Mains switch of
system unit**

**Mains switch of
monitor**

3 You only have to switch on the printer when you need
it. We shall state this explicitly in the exercises.

4 Place the system disk in the 'A' drive. This is usually
the upper drive. Lock the drive using the lever.

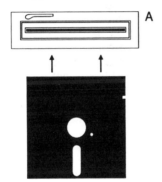

Only use the original disk the very first time you
switch on the computer. Otherwise, use a copy of
the disk to prevent the original disk being damaged
by an accidental manoeuvre. (We shall discuss
how to make a copy of the system disk in sections
4.1 and 4.4.)
In many computers, you can lock the diskdrive before you switch on the computer. It is better not to
do this - the switching on of the flow of electricity in
the mains adapter can cause strong magnetic fields
temporarily which can damage the data on the disk.
Generally, the manufacturer makes drive A the
standard drive. This means that, as a rule, all processing takes place using drive A, unless you spec-

ify another drive. After starting up the computer, you can personally make one of the other drives the current drive. If the computer has a harddisk, this is automatically made the current drive during the starting-up procedure (unless something goes wrong). It receives the name C.

5 The starting-up procedure takes place further automatically. The computer goes through a fixed internal test program which reviews the most important components, particularly the memory and the indispensable peripheral devices.

If, during this test, the computer constitutes a fault, check once more if the connections are in order. Switch off the electricity supply, loosen the cables and connect them once more according to the instructions in the computer handbook. Start up the computer again. If the same fault occurs again, the hardware may be to blame. Look up the meaning of the fault registration in the computer handbook, or approach the supplier or another expert.
You can rectify some disorders yourself:

Releasing hanging (stuck) keys.

Replacing blown fuses. Do not repeat this if the fuse blows again immediately. In this case, expert assistance is necessary.

Defective cables and plugs - you can easily discover this if you have extra cables.

6 After testing itself, the computer will load the most important operating programs from the system disk. This is called *bootload* or *boot.*

If the system disk is not yet in drive A:, or if the locks are still open, the computer will give an error message, for instance:

```
Non-System disk or disk error
Replace and strike any key when ready
```

Place the disk properly in drive A: and press any key. The starting-up process will proceed normally.
This error message will also appear if the disk does not contain system files or if you have accidentally placed the disk in the wrong drive.

7 The rest of the procedure depends upon the commands in the start-up file (AUTOEXEC.BAT). We shall deal with the construction of this file in section 5.5.
Generally, the manufacturer of the system disk makes the disk in such a way that the computer first asks the date and time. (The computer may also have a continuous internal clock.)
Enter the date and time in the same way as shown in the examples. Complete the registration in both cases by pressing Enter.

```
Current date is Tue 01/01/1980
Enter new date (dd-mm-yy): 30-07-1992
Current time is 0:00:54.43
Enter new time: 11:37
```

Possible mistakes: Incorrect registration of the date or time.
Remedy: Repeat registration according to the example.

It is not absolutely necessary to specify the date and/or time. Pressing Enter can also suffice. The computer clock then assumes the system time. (Actually, the clock begins ticking a couple of seconds before the registration is shown on the screen.)
If your computer has a clock which is powered by a battery, you do not need to set the clock. The computer will then bypass these questions (see section 5.4).
We advise you to enter the date and time, since the computer adds this information to the files which

you save on disk. Otherwise it will appear that all files which you make originated on the 1st of January 1980.

It depends on the language of the MS-DOS version which method of date registration the computer expects. Use the English (dd-mm-yy) or the American (mm-dd-yy) methods where required, or adjust, if the MS-DOS version allows this, the language data using a command in the CONFIG.SYS file (see section 6.2).

In the example dealing with the time, we have only entered the hours and minutes. There are very few situations in which the clock has to be synchronized to the exact second, not to mention hundredth of a second. You may try it out if you wish. Type a nice round number and press Enter to coincide with the time signal from the radio or telephone. When dealing with time, you may use a period or a colon as a separation character.

8 The computer continues with the starting-up file and will finally make a statement concerning the DOS type and version. You now operate the computer at the level of the operating system. This is indicated by the A> sign (the prompt). The prompt indicates that the computer is ready to carry out the command which you type at the position of the flashing stripe, the cursor. The dialogue between you and the computer is displayed on the following page.

```
Current date is Tue 01/01/1980
Enter new date (dd-mm-yy): 30-07-92
Current time is 0:00:54.43
Enter new time: 11:37

IBM DOS Version 4.00

A>_
```

Scheme of personal computer starting-up procedure

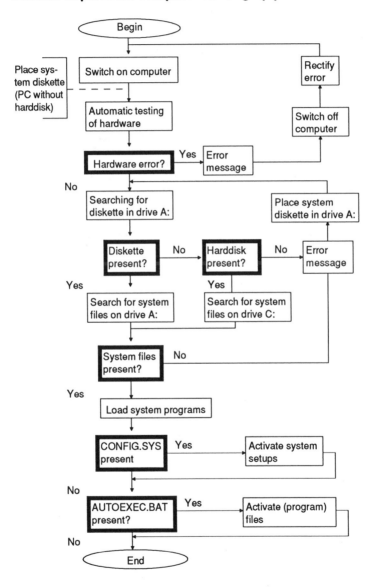

Loading the operating system from the harddisk. If your computer has a harddisk containing the system files, you will have a great deal less work. Ensure that there is no disk in drive A:, since the start procedure always looks for files in drive A: first. If drive A: is not locked, the system will automatically examine the harddisk (drive C:) and will start up from there (see also section 7.1).

Starting the operating system without switching the equipment off and on again. The procedures which we have mentioned above are referred to as the *cold start* or *cold boot*. The computer begins at zero and the electricity supply has to reach the proper levels.
In daily use, all kinds of situations can occur which require you to restart the computer while you are busy with something. Mostly it is a fault in the program which causes the computer to go haywire and to jam (freeze, hang, crash). It is not necessary to use the electricity switches to start up the system again.
By means of a special key combination, the system begins the self-test and the start procedure once more. This is called the *warm start* or *warm boot*.

To implement this warm boot, press the Ctrl and Alt keys simultaneously, hold them down and then press Del.

The keyboard layout differs according to sort and type. On the so-called 'standard' keyboard, Alt, Ctrl and Del occur only once. On the 'extended' keyboard, they each occur twice.

If the system files are not located on the current disk, the computer will give the error message which we discussed above (subsection 6). Open the drive lock if your computer has a harddisk, or place a system disk in the drive.

 In the case of complicated program errors it is occasionally necessary to implement a cold boot. If your computer has a harddisk, you must wait until

the harddisk has stopped completely before switching on again. If not, the start procedure will make a detour along an error treatment routine which will consume unnecessary time (see section 7.1).
In both the cold and the warm boot, the information which was in memory at that moment will be lost. MS-DOS has no RESET instruction which brings a program back to the original state. For this reason, you should always save a new program on disk before you begin trying it out.
Many of the more recent computers do indeed have a reset button, but this does not perform anything more than implement the warm boot in an easy manner.

Interrupting the operating system. Occasionally, the specified command does not lead to the desired result. In this case, there is no sense in waiting until the command has been completely carried out. With MS-DOS you are able to discontinue a procedure by using a key combination.

Interrupt a procedure by simultaneously pressing Ctrl and C or Ctrl and Break.

At the discontinue command, the system returns to DOS. You can then enter a new command behind the prompt.

The key combinations normally only work during procedures dealing with input or implementation of information under DOS. If a program is jammed in a loop which does not deal with these procedures, you will only be able to begin again with a warm boot, or even a cold boot in some rather persistent cases.
In section 6.3, we shall discuss the possibility of extending the scope of the key combinations used for interruption, over and above the procedures concerning normal input and execution.

Interrupting a computer session and stopping the operating system. There is no instruction and no key combination to turn off the operating system.

If you wish to cease working with the computer, proceed as follows:

■ Open all the diskdrives.
■ Switch off the electricity supply of all equipment.

It is much more convenient if all equipment is connected to a junction box. In that case, you only need to remove the plug from the socket and no device will be left on accidentally.

The manufacturers recommend that some devices be switched on and off separately. Conform to the instructions in these cases.

2   MS-DOS basic skills

Entering commands. The MS-DOS operating system is managed using keyboard instructions. The key combinations for a warm boot and for interrupting a process have been discussed in the previous chapter. In this chapter, we shall become familiar with more keys which implement commands in MS-DOS.

Most commands require instructions consisting of more than one letter: these *reserved words* may not be used for other tasks. It makes no difference whether you type the instructions using small letters, capitals or a mixture of both. Internally, MS-DOS works with capitals. The letters which you type appear first on the screen. The text is only passed on to the computer when you complete the input by pressing Enter. Subsequently, the command, if valid, will be implemented.

A command, step by step:

■ Type the command using small letters, capitals or a mixture of these.
■ Complete the command by pressing Enter.
■ The command will appear on the screen at the position of the cursor (insertion point).

Before an instruction, a file name etc. is passed on to the computer you are able to make alterations to it - this is called *editing*. In this, the following keys may be used:

■ To delete a word or a whole line *one character at a time* from right to left: Backspace or cursor left.
■ To delete the entire input requires two steps:
  Step 1: Esc
  Step 2: Enter

The Esc key adds a \(backslash) to the command typed up until now. If you then press Enter the text becomes invalid but does not disappear from the screen. The prompt, A> or C>, indicates that the computer is ready to receive the next command. This method of using Esc works a great deal quicker than repeatedly pressing Backspace (you can hold the key down for automatic repetition of the function).

Example 1: Changing input

```
A:\>diskcopy b: a:                        (1)
    ++++++++++++++++
A:\>diskcopy b: a:\                        (2)
A:\>                                       (3)
```

(1) The entire text is deleted one character at a time using the Backspace key.
(2) The Esc key invalidates the entire text (backslash).
(3) Confirm the backslash by pressing Enter. The text is deleted from the input buffer and the prompt appears again on the screen.

While you type a command, it does not only appear on the screen - it is also retained in a buffer (a help-memory). The command is implemented by the system when you confirm it using Enter.
If you wish to give the same command again immediately, it is not necessary to type it again. You can copy the complete command or parts of it back to the screen. The edit keys which we mentioned above also have an effect on the contents of the buffer.

You can recall the contents of the buffer using the following keys:

F1
Individual character   Copies the contents of the
                                        buffer from the beginning
                                        one character at a time.

F3

Entire command

Copies the entire command from the buffer.

Del

Deletes one character at a time

Deletes the command one character at a time beginning at the cursor position (not visible on the screen!). The shortened text can be copied from the buffer using F1 or F3.

Ins

Inserts characters

Inserts characters at the cursor position. The new characters appear on the screen behind the beginning of the previous command. You may also press Ins immediately. Using F1 or F3, you can copy the (rest of the) text from the buffer.

F2, character

Previous command up to the specified character.

The F2 function key copies the contents *up to* the character specified

F4, character, F3

Previous command from the specified character.

The F4 function key copies the contents of the buffer *from* the character specified. Subsequently, type a new part of the command and add the rest of the buffer contents if required.

Example 2: Altering the command using the function keys

```
A>TYPE B:LETTER.TXT                <1>

A>TYPE                             <2>

A>TYPE B:LETTER.TXT                <3>

A>B:LETTER.TXT                     <4>

A>DIR B:LETTER.TXT                 <5>

A>DIR B:LETTER                     <6>

A>LETTER                           <7>
```

Confirm each step by pressing Enter. This is necessary in order to save the new version of the command in the buffer. This also takes place even if the computer is not able to implement the command because the contents of the command are not valid (see end of Example 2).

(1) This text is still in the buffer from the previous example.
(2) Copy the first word from the buffer by pressing F1 four times.
(3) Copy the rest of the command from the buffer by pressing F3.
(4) Delete the first five characters by pressing Del five times. Copy the rest of the buffer by pressing F3.
(5) Press Ins and type *DIR<space>*. Copy the rest from the buffer by pressing F3.
(6) The command from (5) is in the buffer. Press F2 and then '.' and the contents of the buffer up to the period will appear on the screen.
(7) Press F4 and then on 'L'. Copy the contents of the buffer from the 'L' by pressing F3.

Entering an invalid command. As mentioned, it is not a problem if you give a command which MS-DOS does not understand owing to a typing error or a non-existent file name. The operating system gives an error message and returns to the prompt. Subsequently, you can correct the invalid command in the way dealt with above.

Example 3: Entering an invalid command

```
A:\>disccopy a: b:                        (1)
Bad command or file name                  (2)

A:\>
                                          (3)
```

(1) Invalid command: the command is typed wrongly.
(2) Error message from the operating system.
(3) Prompt.

Implementing commands and program files. For each instruction there is a corresponding program in the MS-DOS operating system. An instruction activates the program of the same name.
Some of these programs are loaded automatically along with the operating system (they are part of the COM-MAND.COM program). For the execution of these *internal commands*, it is not necessary to place the system disk in the current drive.

In order to save memory, the commands which are less frequently used are not included in the 'internal' part of the operating system (the part which is loaded into memory when DOS is loaded). An *external command* activates a program which still has to be loaded from the system disk before it can be implemented. In this case, the disk must be placed in the current drive or there must be a path (see section 7.2) to the directory containing the operating system commands. In section 9.2 we shall further examine the MS-DOS structure.

Besides system programs, you can, of course, load and start up application programs. You will recognize system programs and application programs by their extension:

```
.COM  .EXE  .BAT
```

In order to load and start up a program, it is not neces-sary to specify the extension - the name alone is sufficient. For instance, you can activate the WP.EXE program by using the command WP.

Just as in the case of a DOS instruction, a program will only be implemented when you confirm the command by pressing Enter.

Requesting a program from a disk while the disk is not in the drive. It will undoubtedly occur that you will request a system program or an application while the corresponding disk is not in the specified drive. MS-DOS gives an error message. Discontinue the instruction by pressing A (Abort) or place the proper disk in the drive and press R (Retry) to try again without entering the command again. The F (Fail) or I (Ignore) option is superfluous in this case because the same error message will appear again.

Example 4: Requesting a program from a disk while the disk is not in the specified drive.

```
A:\>b:print binker.bat              (1)

Not ready reading drive B           (2)
Abort, Retry, Fail?a                (3)

A:\>                                (4)
```

(1) Instruction for the print program which is on the disk in drive B:.
(2) The disk is not in the drive - reason for the error message.
(3) Press A (Abort) to discontinue the instruction.
(4) The computer is ready for the following command.

3 The most important commands in MS-DOS

3.1 Switching to another drive

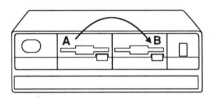

When the operating system has been loaded, the DOS prompt appears on the screen. Generally, the prompt is made up of the current drive letter and a 'greater than' sign. When the computer is started up, the current drive is A or C.
Using a certain command, you can make another drive the current drive, assuming that this drive is available. This is an *internal* command, thus the system disk is not required.

Switch to another standard drive using a command consisting of the new drive letter plus a colon. Confirm the command by pressing Enter.

Command: Switch to another drive

d = drive letter of a chosen harddisk or diskdrive, assuming it is connected.

Example 5: Switching to other drives

```
A:\>b:                                    (1)
B:\>_                                     (2)

B:\>c:                                    (3)
C:\>_

C:\>a:                                    (4)
A:\>_
```

(1) Drive A: is the current drive. Type B and : (without a space between) to switch to drive B:. Confirm the command by pressing Enter.
(2) The computer displays the prompt for drive B:.
(3) Switching from diskdrive B: to C: (harddisk).
(4) Back from the harddisk to drive A:.

Advantage of changing drives. Occasionally, it is necessary to execute a whole series of commands consecutively using programs and/or files from a disk in a drive which is not the standard drive. In this case, you have to explicitly specify the drive in question. Assuming that A: is the current drive, you can activate the PROG program on a disk in drive B: by typing B:PROG. You can place the disk in another drive or make drive B: the current drive (see example 5). The second method is easier and quicker.

3.2   Displaying the directory

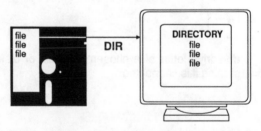

A formatted disk (ready for use) has a data structure in which information is collected concerning the files which are saved on the disk. This data structure is called the *directory.* A directory can be organized into various sub-directories (see section 7.2). Of course, you may only display a directory if the corresponding disk is in the specified drive.

The following command displays the directory from the disk or harddisk specified in the prompt (current drive).

Command: Display directory

```
DIR [/P] [/W]
```

DIR = display directory command
/P   = display directory (screen) page by (screen) page
/W   = display directory wide (in 5 columns)

The parts of the command between the square brackets are optional - you can type them behind the command if required. Do not type the brackets, they are not part of the command.

Example 6: Drive A: is displayed in the prompt. You wish to show the contents of the system disk in this drive on the screen (see diagram following page).

(1) Command to show the directory of the disk in drive A:.
(2) Statement from the operating system: The disk has no name.
(3) List of file names with corresponding information. The files in this example are all operating system programs.
(4) The number of files on the disk and the number of bytes they occupy.
(4a) The memory capacity available.
(5) File names (see section 9.5).
(6) Size of the file in bytes (characters).
(7) Date when last saved.

(8) Time when last saved.

(The size of the system files and the date and time differ according to the MS-DOS version.)

```
A:\>dir                                        (1)

Volume in drive A has no label                 (2)
Volume Serial Number is 2C54-15D6
Directory of A:\

COMMAND  COM     47845 09/04/91    5:00         (3)
4201     CPI      6404 09/04/91    5:00
4208     CPI       720 09/04/91    5:00
5202     CPI       395 09/04/91    5:00
ANSI     SYS      9029 09/04/91    5:00
ANSI33   SYS      1647 24/07/87    0:00
APPEND   EXE     10774 09/04/91    5:00
APPNOTES TXT      9701 09/04/91    5:00
ASSIGN   COM      6399 09/04/91    5:00
ATTRIB   EXE     15796 09/04/91    5:00
BACKUP   EXE     36092 09/04/91    5:00
CHKDSK   EXE     16200 09/04/91    5:00
COMP     EXE     14282 09/04/91    5:00
CONFIG   DU        187 29/07/91   10:22
CONFIG   PM        167 29/07/91   10:22
...
       31 file(s)      591020 bytes            (4)
                       474112 bytes free       (4a)
       (5)        (6)   (7)       (8)
```

If the directory contains more files than there are lines on the screen, the list will shift upwards. This is called *scrolling*. In order to prevent the screen from scrolling, you can have the directory shown page by page (using the /P option). The display halts at the penultimate line on the screen. The message states that the instruction will be further implemented when you press a random key.

Example 7: Displaying a directory page by page (see diagram following page)

(1) Command to display the directory pagewise.
(2) Statement and information as in example 6.
(3) The display stops here - continue by pressing any key.

It is also possible to display the directory without the size and the date and time of saving. In this case, five file names appear on one line. Then there is room on the screen for 80 files. This is mostly sufficient for a quick review of the contents of a disk.

```
A:\>dir /p                                    (1)

   Volume in drive A has no label            (2)
   Volume Serial Number is ZC54-15D6
   Directory of A:\

COMMAND   COM     47845 89/04/91     5:00
4201      CPI      6404 89/04/91     5:00
4208      CPI       720 89/04/91     5:00
5202      CPI       395 89/04/91     5:00
ANSI      SYS      9029 89/04/91     5:00
ANSI33    SYS      1647 24/07/87     0:00
APPEND    EXE     10774 89/04/91     5:00
APPNOTES  TXT      9701 89/04/91     5:00
ASSIGN    COM      6399 89/04/91     5:00
ATTRIB    EXE     15796 89/04/91     5:00
BACKUP    EXE     36892 89/04/91     5:00
CHKDSK    EXE     16200 89/04/91     5:00
COMP      EXE     14282 89/04/91     5:00
CONFIG    DU        187 29/07/91    10:22
CONFIG    PM        167 29/07/91    10:22
CONFIG    UDI       251 07/08/91    12:30
CONFIG    UP        174 29/07/91    10:23
CONFIG    UPP       148 10/01/92    12:46
Press any key to continue . . .               (3)
```

Example 8: Display the directory wide

```
A:\>dir /w                                                          (1)

   Volume in drive A has no label                                   (2)
   Volume Serial Number is ZC54-15D6
   Directory of A:\

COMMAND.COM      4201.CPI        4208.CPI       5202.CPI      ANSI.SYS      (3)
ANSI33.SYS       APPEND.EXE      APPNOTES.TXT   ASSIGN.COM    ATTRIB.EXE
BACKUP.EXE       CHKDSK.EXE      COMP.EXE       CONFIG.DU     CONFIG.PM
CONFIG.UDI       CONFIG.UP       CONFIG.UPP     CONFIG.WIN    COUNTRY.SYS
DEBUG.EXE        DELOLDOS.EXE    DISKCOMP.COM   DISKCOPY.COM  DISPLAY.SYS
DOSHELP.HLP      DOSKEY.COM      DOSSHELL.COM   DOSSHELL.EXE  DOSSHELL.GRB
DOSSHELL.HLP
        31 file(s)      591020 bytes
                        474112 bytes free
```

(1) Command for wide display.
(2) Statement as in examples 6 and 7.
(3) File names in five columns.

It is not necessary to switch to another drive if the disk containing the desired directory is not in the current drive. Specify the corresponding drive letter with a colon in the command.

Example 9: There are various possibilities to request the directory of a disk which is not in the current drive.

```
A:\>dir b:                          (1)
A:\>dir c:
A:\>dir b:/u
A:\>dir c:/p

B:\>dir a:                          (2)
B:\>dir a:/u

C:\>dir a:                          (3)
C:\>dir b:/p
```

(1) Drive A: is the current drive. You wish to see the directories of various drives and harddisks without having to switch. The /P and /W options have the functions already mentioned.
(2) As in (1), but in this case from drive B:.
(3) As in (1), from C:.

Displaying part of a directory. The method of specification of file names must conform to certain rules (see section 9.5). Instead of registering the file names and typing in the full name you can replace parts of the name by the * and ? characters, so-called 'wildcards'.
Imagine that, of all the files on a disk, you only wish to see the BASIC programs in the directory. Or perhaps you wish to find out if the same file name occurs with different extensions, or you wish to know which is the last file in a series of files with a number in the name.

Example 10: Displaying a selection from the directory with the help of wildcards

```
A:\>dir *.bas                       (1)

A:\>dir b:*.txt                     (2)

A:\>dir try.*                       (3)

A:\>dir c:table.*                   (4)

C:\>dir b:letter??.*                (5)
```

These commands will produce the the following lists of files:

(1) All file names with the extension .BAS (BASIC program).

(2) All file names with the extension .TXT (text files) on the disk in drive B:.

(3) All file names which begin with TRY with any extension.

(4) All file names which begin with TABLE with any extension, which are on the harddisk.

(5) All file names on drive B: which begin with LETTER plus any two other characters and which have any extension.

3.3   Interrupting or ending screen display

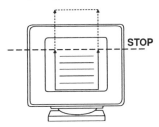

Stopping rolling screen display. Long directories do not fit into the screen. In addition to the /P option, there is also another method to interrupt the screen display in order to gain the chance to read the directory.

The key combination Ctrl+NumLock or the Pause key on its own (depending on the keyboard used) stops the display. Pressing any key resumes the display at the point of interruption.

Example 11: Stopping the rolling screen

```
A:\>dir                                    (1)

 Volume in drive A has no label            (2)
 Volume Serial Number is 2C54-15D6
 Directory of A:\

COMMAND   COM     47845 09/04/91    5:00
4201      CPI      6404 09/04/91    5:00
4208      CPI       720 09/04/91    5:00
5202      CPI       395 09/04/91    5:00
ANSI      SYS      9029 09/04/91    5:00
ANSI33    SYS      1647 24/07/87    0:00
APPEND    EXE     10774 09/04/91    5:00
APPNOTES  TXT      9701 09/04/91    5:00
ASSIGN    COM      6399 09/04/91    5:00
ATTRIB    EXE     15796 09/04/91    5:00
BACKUP    EXE     36092 09/04/91    5:00
CHKDSK    EXE     16200 09/04/91    5:00
COMP      EXE     14282 09/04/91    5:00
CONFIG    DU        187 29/07/91   10:22
CONFIG    PM        167 29/07/91   10:22
CONFIG    VDI       251 07/08/91   12:30
CONFIG    UP                                (3)
```

(1) Command to display the directory.
(2) Statement and information as in previous examples.
(3) The moment of the Pause key. The display continues from this point after pressing any key.

Ending screen display. If the information you require
is located at the beginning of the screen display, you
can cancel the rest.

**You can end the screen display by using the key
combinations Ctrl+C and Ctrl+Break**

The operating system returns to the prompt. You can
enter a new command immediately.

Example 12: Ending screen display

```
A:\>dir                                    (1)

 Volume in drive A has no label           (2)
 Volume Serial Number is 2C54-15D6
 Directory of A:\

COMMAND   COM    47845 09/04/91   5:00
4201      CPI     6404 09/04/91   5:00
4208      CPI      720 09/04/91   5:00
5202      CPI      395 09/04/91   5:00
ANSI      SYS     9829 09/04/91   5:00
ANSI33    SYS     1647 24/07/87   0:00
APPEND    EXE    10774 09/04/91   5:00
APPNOTES  TXT     9701 09/04/91   5:00
^C                                         (3)

A:\>_
```

(1) Command to display directory.
(2) Statement and information as in previous examples.
(3) The display position at the moment of key combination Ctrl+Break (same effect as Ctrl+C).

3.4 Clearing the screen display

The CLS command, confirmed with Enter, clears the current screen display. Subsequently, only the prompt is shown on the screen (upper left-hand corner). It is an internal command - it activates an *internal system program* - thus, the system disk is not needed.

The CLS command clears the current screen display.

Command: Clear screen

CLS = clear screen

Example 13: Clear screen

```
A:\>dir                              (1)

   Volume in drive A has no label
   Volume Serial Number is 2C54-15D6
   Directory of A:\

COMMAND   COM     47845 09/04/91     5:00
4201      CPI      6404 09/04/91     5:00
4208      CPI       720 09/04/91     5:00
5202      CPI       395 09/04/91     5:00
ANSI      SYS      9029 09/04/91     5:00
ANSI33    SYS      1647 24/07/87     0:00
APPEND    EXE     10774 09/04/91     5:00
APPNOTES  TXT      9701 09/04/91     5:00
^C

A:\>cls_                             (2)
```

(1) Command, statement, information and discontinuation as in previous examples.

(2) Command to clear screen. Just as with other commands, CLS must also be confirmed by pressing Enter.

3.5   Printing the screen display

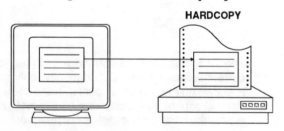

HARDCOPY

Transporting the current screen contents to the printer. If you have connected a printer to the computer, you can print the current contents of the screen (data shown on the monitor) using the printer. The printer copies the contents of the screen, in as much as the printer is able to reproduce the characters. This printed copy is called a *hardcopy*.

Check the following points before giving the print command:
Is the printer connected?
Is there paper in the printer?
Is the printer switched on?
Is the printer ON LINE (ready)?

The Shift+PrintScreen key combination transports the current screen display to the printer. (On extended keyboards PrintScreen is sufficient.)

You may repeat this command as often as you like.

On some keyboards the lettering on the print key is PrtSc or Print. If that is not the case, consult your handbook.

Types of printers. Not all printers are able to print all the characters shown on the screen. A daisy wheel printer is only able to print characters which occur on the wheel, mostly only the alphanumeric characters which are also used on a typewriter.
Printers which construct the letters in another way using points (needle or matrix printer, laser printer, inkjet printer) can reproduce all the screen characters if they are connected to the computer by a suitable interface. This also applies to drawings on the screen. These kinds of printers are also called graphic printers. In addition, there are also printers for coloured images. These require a special interface.

Printing the contents of a colour graphics screen. If your computer has a graphic monitor, linked to the computer via a colour graphics adapter, a special *external system program* is needed to make a screendump (hardcopy). (Don't forget to place the system disk in the current drive.)

**The graphic print program transports a graphic
screen to the printer.**

Command: Activate the Screendump function for a
graphic screen.

```
GRAPHICS
```

GRAPHICS = drawings, pictures

You only need to give the GRAPHICS command once.
The program remains in memory as long as the computer is on. If you include this activation in the start program, you will not have to concern yourself further with
starting up this program (see section 5.5).

3.6 Reproducing the screen contents on the printer

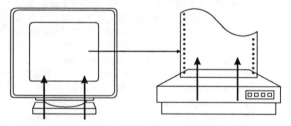

The flow of data from the computer to the screen can
also be simultaneously reproduced on the printer. You
can then examine in retrospect what you have done.
This is useful, for instance, for making a protocol if you
are testing a program. You can also use this function to
reproduce a long directory or text on paper as well as
on the screen.

First check if the printer is ready (see section 3.5).

The Ctrl+PrintScreen key combination ensures that the data flow of a command is transported not only to the screen but also to the printer.
If you repeat this key combination, you disconnect the printer again.

You can switch the protocol function on and off as often as you wish. It has no influence upon the data flow, apart from the fact that information is transported to the screen a little slower. This takes place at the pace of the printer. If you activate this function when the printer is not ready, the computer will give an error message. You can only continue when you have adjusted the printer properly, or after a warm or cold restart.

3.7   Transporting the contents of a file to the screen or the printer

Displaying the contents of a file on the screen. You can not only request the names of the files on a disk, you can also request the contents of the file. This is useful if you no longer know the contents of the file, if you are searching for certain information in a file, or if you only wish to review the contents of the file.

Only files with alphanumeric contents are legible (ASCII format). This may be a normal text or a non-compiled program (source text with non-compiled commands). It is possible to transport the contents of a program in computer language to the screen, but you will then see a hotch-potch of strange characters with here and there a letter or a number (see section 9.5).

The TYPE command activates an *internal system program* - thus, the system disk is not needed.

Specify behind the command and the space the complete name of the file you wish to examine.
If the file is located on a disk other than the current one, you must also specify the proper drive.

Command: Display the contents of a file.

```
TYPE [d:]file.ext
```

TYPE   = type
d: = letter of the drive with the disk upon
                which the file is located
file.ext   = name of the file (including extension)

With the TYPE command, the * and ? wildcards are not
valid.

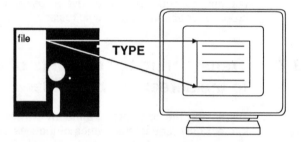

Example 14: The LETTER.TXT file which is to be displayed on the screen is located on the disk in drive B:.

```
A:\>type b:letter.txt                                    (1)

Dear Sir,                                                (2)
     As a loving and disquieted parent, I would like to
express my concern over the recent upsurge in joyriding. In
addition to general condemnation of this practice, perhaps
society can also take more preventative steps. Television
pictures show that joyriders seldom use the indicators and it
might be a good idea to give children at school a course in the
use of good old-fashioned hand signals. I would also recommend
that aeroplanes and submarines be wrapped in heavy chains at
night. I do not relish the thought of evil-smelling packages
being thrown down my chimney by irresponsible brats terrorising
the skies or the foundations of our beautiful beaches, which we
have defended so heroically against the Romans, Huns, Eskimos and
oilslicks, being battered by uneducated louts. My thirteen-year-
old son ensures me that it is quite easy to steal a car, thus I
would argue the case for compulsory tyre deflation at night and
each house being supplied with a compressed-air cylinder. After
all, where does our road tax go?
                         Yours faithfully,
                         Billy Binkerhill (Mrs.)

A:\>
```

(1) The command to show the file. Do not forget to specify the drive and the extension.

(2) The TYPE command does indeed show the text literally, but the original formatting characters (layout codes) are omitted. Only the characters for 'end paragraph' and the Tabs are retained.

If, using the TYPE command, you display a file which has been created using a word-processing program such as WORD or WordPerfect, you will see all sorts of characters which are invisible in the word processor - break codes, italics, underlining etc.

Due to the fact that these codes are very specific, you will generally have to remove them if you wish to continue using the text in another way. Most word-processors have an option enabling you to save text without the layout codes (excepting paragraphs and tabs) - in the so-called ASCII format.

If you wish to review the scheme of a BASIC program using the TYPE command, this is only functional if you have explicitly saved the source text from the BASIC interpreter in the alphanumeric format. (Normally, this takes place in a coded form, allowing the program to be implemented quicker.) This is done using the *,A* command - referring to ASCII format when saving:

```
SAVE program,A
```

Displaying a file pagewise on the screen. In the same way as with DIR/P, you can also display the contents of a file page by page on the screen. It would be rather tedious to have to press the Pause key after each page in order to get the chance to read the text.

If you extend the TYPE command with the pipe symbol |, the data requested by the TYPE command is transported via a metaphorical pipe to the following command. In this case, that is the MORE instruction, which is a kind of line counter. The contents of the file no longer roll over the screen - they stop at the last screen line. The statement '--More--' is shown there. To display the following page, you only have to press a random key.

The MORE command is an *external command* - you can only make use of it if the system disk is located in the current drive or if you are working with a harddisk (see chapter 7).

The following command displays the contents of a file pagewise on the screen.

Command: display file pagewise on the screen

```
TYPE [d:]file.ext|MORE
```

MORE   = more
| = vertical, broken stripe
                The pipe symbol is available on most
                keyboards. If this is not the case, you
                can create it using an Alt key combina-
                tion - hold down the Alt key and press
                consecutively the numbers 1,2 and 4
                on the numeric keypad at the right-
                hand side of the keyboard (124 is the
                ASCII code for the pipe symbol).

Example 15: Displaying a file pagewise on the screen

```
A:\>type b:letter.txt|more                              (1)

Dear Sir,
        As a loving and disquieted parent, I would like to
express my concern over the recent upsurge in joyriding. In
addition to general condemnation of this practice, perhaps
society can also take more preventative steps. Television
pictures show that joyriders seldom use the indicators and it
might be a good idea to give children at school a course in the
use of good old-fashioned hand signals. I would also recommend
that aeroplanes and submarines be wrapped in heavy chains at
night. I do not relish the thought of evil-smelling packages
being thrown down my chimney by irresponsible brats terrorising
the skies or the foundations of our beautiful beaches, which we
have defended so heroically against the Romans, Huns, Eskimos and
oilslicks, being battered by uneducated louts. My thirteen-year-
old son ensures me that it is quite easy to steal a car, thus I
would argue the case for compulsory tyre deflation at night and
each house being supplied with a compressed-air cylinder. After
all, where does our road tax go?
...
...
...
...
-- More --                                              (2)
```

(1) Extended display command.
(2) This statement appears at the bottom of the screen. Press a random key to show the following page.

Reproducing the contents of a file using the printer.
In this book, we shall discuss two possibilities.

■ Displaying a file using the protocol mode.
■ Displaying a file using a special DOS command.

Possibility no.1

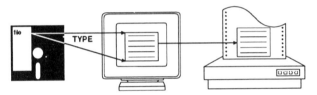

We have already dealt with simultaneous reproduction on screen and printer in section 3.6. We shall summarize once more, paying attention to the current subject matter.

The following three manoeuvres (also) reproduce a file on the printer:

1 Activate the protocol function for the printer using Ctrl+PrintScreen.

2 Transport the contents of the file to the screen:

Command: Display the contents of a file.

```
TYPE [d:]file.ext
```

The file is now not only shown on the screen, it is also reproduced on the printer because the protocol function is active.

3   Switch off the protocol function once more by pressing Ctrl+PrintScreen.

Possibility no.2

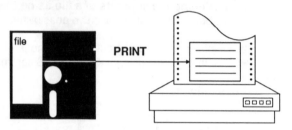

MS-DOS contains an *external system program* which transports the contents of a file to the printer without having to activate the protocol function for the printer. In this case, the system disk is needed.

Transporting the contents of a file to the printer alone.

Command: transport the file contents to the printer

```
PRINT [d:]file.ext
```

PRINT   = print
d: = letter of the drive containing the file
file.ext   = name of the file to be printed

The * and ? wildcards are valid in the PRINT command.

The contents of the file are transported to the printer, *not* to the screen.
The first time you give a PRINT command when you have switched on the computer, the system will ask the name of the printer. Confirm the standard name PRN using Enter or type another name if you have installed another printer, LPT1, for example. In all subsequent instances, the PRINT command will be implemented (as long as you have not switched off the computer).

Example 16: Print the text files LETTER10 and INFO.TXT from the disk in drive B:

```
A:\>print b:\letter10.txt                    (1)
Name of list device [PRN]:                    (2)
Resident part of PRINT installed              (3)


  B:\LETTER10.TXT is currently being printed  (4)

A:\>print b:\info.txt                         (5)


  B:\INFO.TXT is currently being printed      (6)
```

(1) PRINT command for the LETTER10 file on a disk in drive B:.
(2) The PRINT command prompt for the name of the list device. If the printer is connected to the standard interface for the printer, you only need to press Enter.
(3) Part of the PRINT program remains available in memory. It becomes *resident.*
(4) Statement: The command is carried out.
(5) The second PRINT command, now for the B:INFO.TXT file.
(6) The PRINT statement for the second file.

More about the PRINT command

The two methods of printing files have their own area of application.
The TYPE internal command with the protocol function is useful for short files and has the advantage that the system disk is not necessary.
The PRINT external command has benefits when dealing with longer files, and is also advantageous if you wish to print several files consecutively using one command. While the PRINT command is being executed, you can use the computer for other tasks.

The PRINT command in MS-DOS has two exceptional features:

■ The PRINT command can print a file *in the back-ground*- in other words, you can use the computer for other jobs in the meantime (in the foreground). Due to the fact that the computer cannot really implement two jobs simultaneously, it switches rapidly between these two activities. A task in the foreground is ex-ecuted noticably slower - in the case of displaying (another) file on the screen, for instance.

■ You may register several file names in one go behind the PRINT command. The names are recorded in a queue, and the files are printed consecutively. As long as the computer is busy with printing, you can add files to, or remove them from, the queue.

When printing a queue, the following preconditions apply:

■ The printer is ready.
■ The files named are located on the specified disk.
■ The printer is not available for other commands while dealing with the queue.

The PRINT queue. You may register a *maximum of ten* files behind the PRINT command:

```
PRINT file1.ext file2.ext ... filen.ext
```

The files are printed in the registered order of se-quence. Normally, *n* is a maximum of 10.

The add mode, /P:

```
PRINT file.ext[/P]
```

The FILE.EXT file is added to the existing queue and is printed when its turn comes around. The /P option is standard: you only need to state this option if you have already removed a file from the queue.

The delete mode, /C:

```
PRINT file1.ext/C file2.ext ...
```

The file with the /C option (cancel) disappears from the queue. This applies to all files behind this option. If one of these files is being printed at that moment, the command will break off the execution with the message:

```
File.ext file cancelled by operator
```

The printer gives an alarm signal and the paper moves on to the next sheet. You can then switch the PRINT command over again to the add mode using the PRINT /P file.ext command (see above).

Breaking off the PRINT command:

```
PRINT /T
```

The /T option (terminate) removes the print queue and breaks off the PRINT command with the statement:

```
All files cancelled by operator
```

The printer gives a warning and the paper moves on to the next sheet.

Displaying the current contents of the queue:

```
PRINT
```

A list of the files in the queue appears on the screen along with the file which is being printed at that moment.

Example 17: Using the queue to print several files

```
A:\>print letter.txt advert.123 request.dat

  A:\LETTER.TXT is currently being printed
  A:\ADVERT.123 is in queue
  A:\REQUEST.DAT is in queue

A:\>print order.opd

  A:\LETTER.TXT is currently being printed
  A:\ADVERT.123 is in queue
  A:\REQUEST.DAT is in queue
  A:\ORDER.OPD is in queue

A:\>print request.dat/c opder.opd action.305/p

  A:\LETTER.TXT is currently being printed
  A:\ADVERT.123 is in queue
  A:\ACTION.305 is in queue

A:\>print

  A:\ACTION.305 is currently being printed

A:\>print /t
PRINT queue is empty
```

(1) The LETTER.TXT, ADVERT.123 and RE-
QUEST.DAT files are registered in the queue and subsequently printed.

(2) The ORDER.OPD file is added to the queue.

(3) The REQUEST.DAT and ORDER.OPD files are
removed from the queue. ACTION.305 is added. No
break-off message is shown because neither of the
removed files was being printed at that moment.

(4) Implements the current contents of the queue. It is
obvious that only the file which is being printed at this
moment is still in the list.

(5) The command completes the printing of the only file
still in the list. The queue has been processed and the
command states that the queue is empty.

The printer registers a break-off message for the last
file, gives a warning signal and moves the paper on to
the following sheet.

3.8 Exercises

1 Start up the computer using the system disk in drive A:.

2 Place another disk containing files in drive B:.

3 Request the directory of the disk in drive B: without switching over to this drive.

4 Make drive B: the current drive and request the directory of the disk in this drive.

5 Switch the operating system over to drive A: once more, and display the directory of the system disk in three ways - standard, pagewise and wide.

6 Request the names of only those files on the system disk with the .COM extension. Use the * wildcard (consult the last part of section 9.5 for examples if necessary).

7 Display the names of all files which begin with the letter C. Use the ? and * wildcards.

8 Transport the current contents of the screen to the printer.

4   File management on floppies and harddisk

The operating system manages programs and information in the form of files. You can only retain files in the computer memory as long as the computer is switched on. In order to save them permanently, the files have to be saved in an external memory - on floppies or on a harddisk upon which information is stored magnetically. You must personally organize this management, assisted by the operating system:

■ ensure that diskettes are available
■ prepare the diskettes (format them)
■ make reserve copies (backups)   .
■ check storage media and files and delete when necessary
■ correct errors.

We shall discuss the management functions for the storage media in this chapter. If you have very little experience of this, it is advisable to first read sections 9.4 and 9.5 which deal with diskettes and file names.
Some instructions only apply to floppies - we shall state this explicitly. Others refer also to the harddisk.
The instructions in this chapter should lead to few insurmountable problems and if anything in a command is not quite correct, the system will give a clear error message. The only possible risk lurks in instructions which delete files, but we shall deal extensively with this at the proper place.

4.1   Copying an entire diskette

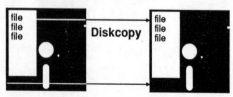

In the simplest method of making a copy of a diskette,
the contents of the original diskette (*source diskette*) are
copied in the same order of sequence, one character at
a time, to the new diskette (*target diskette*).

In most versions of MS-DOS, even if the target diskette
has not been used previously, it is generally not necessary to prepare this diskette (formatting, see section 4.3).
The DISKCOPY copying program, which copies complete *diskettes*, does this automatically if required. (The
COPY command copies one or more complete *files*
(see section 4.4) - this command only works with a formatted target diskette.)

Both programs can be run with either one or two diskdrives. With two diskdrives, it is not necessary to switch
the source and target diskettes.

If the target diskette still contains files, the copy program will overwrite these. Accordingly, the original
information is irretrievably lost.
Pay special attention to whether the target diskette
has already been used or has already been formatted: do not place this diskette in the wrong drive
(read drive). This automatically entails that the
source diskette will be placed in the write drive: you
will then lose your data. The copy program cannot
see which diskette you wish to use as the source
diskette and which is the target diskette - no error
message will be given if you make a mistake here!
You can protect the source diskette against unintentional overwriting by placing a sticker over the
write-protection slot.
The copy program only works with media of the
same type - not from diskette to harddisk, and not
from a 5.25 diskette to a 3.5 diskette and vice
versa.

The copy program is an external command. The system
diskette has to be placed in the current drive first.

The DISKCOPY command copies the contents of a diskette to a new diskette, without any alteration.

Command: Copy diskette

```
DISKCOPY [d1:] [d2:] [/1]
```

d1:   = source drive
d2:   = target drive
/1   = copy only one side

When the copy program has been loaded, it asks you to place the source diskette in the drive represented by *d1:* and the target diskette in the drive represented by *d2:*. In principle, it makes no difference if you specify the order of sequence as being A-B or B-A, but in order to avoid mistakes, it is advisable to employ always the same order of sequence.

Example 18: Copy the contents of a diskette in drive A: to a new diskette in drive B:

```
A:\>diskcopy a: b:                      (1)

Insert SOURCE diskette in drive A:      (2)

Press any key to continue . . .

Copying 40 tracks                       (3)
9 sectors per track, 2 side(s)

Insert TARGET diskette in drive B:      (4)

Press any key to continue . . .

Formatting while copying                (5)

Volume Serial Number is 16FZ-0A58

Copy another diskette (Y/N)? n          (6)

A:\>                                     (7)
```

(1) The command loads the copy program into memory and activates it.
(2) The program gives a prompt to place the source disk-

ette in the specified first drive. You may place the target diskette in drive B: to avoid mistakes. The program will begin copying as soon as you press a key.

(3) The program states that it has loaded both sides of the diskette, each containing 40 tracks of 9 sectors, into the computer memory.

(4) The program asks you to place the target diskette in drive B:, even if it is already located there. Press Enter to continue.

(5) The program registers that the target diskette is un-formatted and states that the diskette will be processed during copying.

(6) The program asks if you wish to copy another disk-ette: an identical copy or a copy of another diskette. That is not our intention at the moment. Answer N (No).

(7) By answering N, the DISKCOPY program is ended and MS-DOS resumes operation. The prompt makes this evident.

If you omit both drives from the command, the program will only work with the current drive. This is the case, for instance, if your computer only has one diskdrive. The program uses the computer memory as a buffer for the data to be copied. The frequency of switching between source and target diskette depends upon the amount of memory in your computer and the type of diskettes.

Example 19: Variations in the copy command

```
A:\>diskcopy            (1)

B:\>diskcopy            (2)

A:\>diskcopy a:         (3)

A:\>diskcopy b:         (4)

C:\>diskcopy a: a:      (5)

A:\>diskcopy a: b:/1    (6)
```

(1) The command only uses A:, the current diskdrive. The source drive and the target drive are the same. The program states when the diskettes should be switched.

(2) As in (1), but now from B:.

(3) As in (1). The drive first specified is always interpreted as being the source drive. Because this is the same as the current drive, this addition does not change anything.

(4) The source drive is B:, the target drive is A:. The contents of the diskette in B: are copied to the diskette in A:.

(5) The copy program is loaded and started up from the harddisk. Just as with (1), A: is both source and target drive.

(6) The /1 option ensures that the copy program only copies side 1 of the source diskette to side 1 of the target diskette. This is an obsolete option, which dates from the time that diskdrives had only one write head.

Advanced users make mistakes in giving commands now and again, just as beginners do. This is generally not serious, since the system will state in one way or another that the instruction is not correct. The following example illustrates the effect of various mistakes.

Example 20: Error message in the DISKCOPY command

```
A:\>dskcopy a: b:
Bad command or file name                      (1)

C:\>diskcopy a:

Invalid drive specification                   (2)
Specified drive does not exist
or is non-removable

A:\>diskcopy a: b:

Insert SOURCE diskette in drive A:

Insert TARGET diskette in drive B:

Press any key to continue . . .
Not ready - A:                                (3)
Make sure a diskette is inserted into
the drive and the door is closed

Press CTRL+C to abort,
or correct this problem and press any other key to continue . . .

Write protect error                           (4)
```

(1) Error: The command is wrongly written.
Remedy: type again, or alter using the input buffer: F2, S, Ins, I, F3.
(2) Error: The command copies the contents of A: to the harddisk. (The target drive does not exist or is non-re-movable.)
Remedy: Switch to drive A:. (If, due to this, this system files on C are no longer available, you can activate the copy program by typing A>C:DISKCOPY.)
(3) Error: The diskette is not yet located in the specified drive or the drive is not yet locked.
(4) Error: The write-protection slot has been taped over (in the case of a 3.5 inch diskette, the small sleeve is open).
Remedy: Check if you still require the files. If not, remove the tape (or close the sleeve), otherwise use another diskette.

The copy program may occasionally write informa-tion from the source diskette over a part of COM-MAND.COM in the computer memory. That part has to be reloaded from the system diskette when DISKCOPY is completed. This is not noticeable in the case of a harddisk, but if your computer only has diskdrives, the so-called 'resident portion' of COMMAND.COM will give a message:

```
Invalid COMMAND.COM
Insert disk with COMMAND.COM in drive A:
Press any key to continue...
```

Place the system diskette in the current drive and press a key to reload COMMAND.COM.

If the operating system does not accept the DISK-COPY command, the program in your version may have another name - DSKCOPY, for instance. Alter the command, or give the program another name by using the RENAME option (see section 4.8).

Files which you frequently use and alter remain an entity as regards administration, but they become more fragmented on the diskette with the passage of time. Loading and saving them becomes ever more time-consuming. The situation remains unchanged if you copy files using DISKCOPY. By using COPY (section 4.4), you can make the files an entity again on the target diskette.

4.2   Comparing diskettes

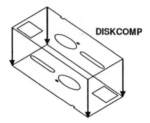

The DISKCOMP command enables you to:

■ compare copies of diskettes to each other and to the original
■ trace faults in copies.

Use of this command is highly recommended if you wish to be sure that the copy of a diskette containing indispensable information is identical to the original. The DISKCOMP command is only serviceable in the case of diskettes which have been copied using DISKCOPY. To compare a single file or a group of files, the COMP command is available (section 4.5).

The DISKCOMP command can only be used for diskettes. If you attempt to compare the contents of a diskette to the contents of a harddisk, you will receive an error message.

The command activates an external program which compares the copy, track by track, to the original. A message specifies each deviation. Possible causes of such messages are:

- Something has gone wrong during the copying process. Perhaps the copy contains damaged tracks or
  sectors.
- If both diskettes are copies, perhaps one has been
  made using COPY. Then the files are written differently on to the diskette.
- You have altered something on the copy or on the
  original before the comparison.
- The files on the diskettes are completely different.

You can attempt to correct copy errors by copying the
original diskette to the target diskette once more. If, at
the following comparison, the diskettes still differ, the
conclusion is that the target diskette cannot be used
with DISKCOPY. Do not immediately throw the diskette
away - it can be useful, when formatted again, for storing odd files. If the format program states that the diskette contains unserviceable sectors, the diskette is not
in order. If you format the diskette again, it may help, but
if the trouble persists, you will not be able to use the
diskette.

DISKCOMP is an *external system program*: the system
diskette needs to be placed in the current drive.

**The DISKCOMP instruction compares the contents
of two diskettes.**

Command: Compare diskettes

```
DISKCOMP d1: d2: [/1] [/8]
```

d1:   = name of the first diskdrive
d2:   = name of the second diskdrive

        Special options (see also DISKCOPY).

/1   = compares only the first sides of the diskettes
/8   = compares only the first eight sectors of each
         track

It is possible to compare two diskettes using one diskdrive. The program then states when the diskettes have
to be switched.

Example 21: Comparison of two identical diskettes in
different diskdrives

```
A:\>diskcomp a: b:                      (1)

Insert FIRST diskette in drive A:       (2)

Press any key to continue . . .

Comparing 40 tracks                     (3)
9 sectors per track, 2 side(s)

Insert SECOND diskette in drive B:      (4)

Press any key to continue . . .

Compare OK                              (5)

Compare another diskette (Y/N) ?n       (6)

A:\>
```

(1) Command to compare the diskettes in drives A: and
B:.
(2) The prompt asks you to place the first diskette in
drive A: and then to press any key.
(3) The program registers the diskette features.
(4) The prompt asks you to place the second diskette in
B: and then to press any key.
(5) The program states that the two diskettes are identical.
(6) The program asks if you wish to compare more diskettes. Discontinue the program with N (Enter is not
necessary).

Example 22: Comparison of two differing diskettes in
one diskdrive (A:) (see diagram following page)

(1) Due to the fact that the comparison takes place in
one diskdrive (current), it is not necessary to specify the
diskdrives.

```
A:\>diskcomp a: b:                      (1)

Insert FIRST diskette in drive A:       (2)

Press any key to continue . . .

Comparing 40 tracks                     (3)
9 sectors per track, 2 side(s)

Insert SECOND diskette in drive B:      (4)

Press any key to continue . . .

Compare error on                        (5)
side 0, track 10
       .
       .
       .
Compare error on
side 1, track 39

Compare another diskette (Y/N) ?n       (6)

A:\>
```

(2) (3) The statements and prompts are similar to those in example 21.
(4) Replace the first diskette with the second one.
(5) The program registers a whole series of deviations along with the track and sectors in which these are located. Owing to shortage of space, we have omitted most of these.
(6) As in example 21.

4.3   Formatting diskettes

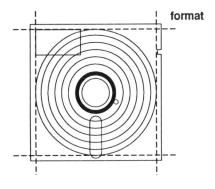

format

Two types of diskette are in use: 5.25 inch and 3.5 inch.
(In the past the 8 inch disk was also used.) Both types
are available with two sorts of magnetic layers, *high
density* (HD) and *double density* (DD). The storage capacity of HD diskettes is far greater than that of the DD
type. Nowadays, all diskettes are written on both sides
(double-sided, DS).

A new diskette has to be prepared to be able to save
files in an orderly way, so that they can easily be recalled. The format program writes concentric tracks on
the diskette, each of these tracks being divided into a
fixed number of sectors. In addition, on the first track,
the program creates a book-keeping system for the file
names and a table where the file blocks are located, the
file allocation table (FAT).

The DISKCOPY copy program is an exception, due to
the fact that, in most MS-DOS versions, it formats the
diskette itself if necessary. It has been specially constructed to facilitate making reserve copies of diskettes.
The formatting program which we are discussing in this
section is a part of DISKCOPY.

The formatting program deletes *all* data from the
diskette or harddisk (!) specified in the command.
Check if you have specified the correct (disk)drive
before confirming the command. The effect of a format command cannot be undone!
Never give the format command without specifying
the diskdrive.
Read section 7.1 before formatting the harddisk.

The formatting program is an *external system program* -
it has to be loaded from the system disk in the current
drive.

**The FORMAT command prepares a diskette or
harddisk for storage of information.**

Command: Format diskette/harddisk

```
FORMAT [d:] [/S] [/V]
       [/1] [/8] [/4] [U]
       [/T:aa] [/N:bb]
```

d: = drive specified in the format command
/S   = copy, in addition, the most important system
        programs
/V   = ask, at completion, for a name for the disk-
        ette/harddisk

Structural deviations (for diskettes only)

/1   = format one side
/8   = make 8 instead of 9 sectors per track
/B   = format 8 sectors per track and reserve space
        in order to be able to add the system files later
        (not allowed using /S and/or /V).
/4   = format a 5,25 inch DD-diskette in a HD-disk-
        drive (from MS-DOS version 3.0 onwards; read
        section 9.4 first)
/U   = (version 5 only) unconditional format, which
        destroys all data on the target disk to prevent
        subsequent unformatting with the UNFORMAT
        command
/T:aa = Make AA tracks.

Example: The number of tracks for a 3.5-inch DD-diskette (720 Kb) in a HD-diskdrive (capacity 1.44 Mb) is 80.

/N:bb = Make BB sectors per track. In the example
        above, bb=9.
        Note: /T:aa and /N:bb must *both* be specified al-
        ways.

Example 23: Formatting diskette

```
A:\>format  a:/4 /u                    (1)
Insert new diskette for drive A:       (2)
and press ENTER when ready...

39 percent completed.                  (3)
Format complete.                       (4)
Volume label (11 characters, ENTER for none)?

    362496 bytes total disk space      (5)
    362496 bytes available on disk

      1024 bytes in each allocation unit.
       354 allocation units available on disk.

Volume Serial Number is 2423-17DB

Format another (Y/N)?n                 (6)


A:\>
```

(1) This command loads the format program. It is not really necessary to specify the target drive because this is
the current drive in this case.
(2) The program only continues when you have placed
another diskette in the specified (or current) drive. Confirm this using Enter.
(3) The stages of the formatting process are registered.
(4) The previous statement is replaced by the statement
that the command is completed.
(5) The program states the created and the available
storage capacity. Between these two lines the number
of defective sectors, if any, will be stated (these will be
automatically blocked), along with the capacity occupied by the system files (see also example 24).
(6) Finally, the program will ask if you wish to format another disk. If you respond *N, Enter.* the program will be
closed and you will return to the prompt.

The /S option, copying system programs. In order to
be able to start up any program, the operating system
files must be available to the computer. In a roundabout
way, you can achieve this by first starting up the computer using the system diskette and then loading the required program from another diskette.

You are able to start up the computer using the program diskette if this has been equipped with the most important system files during formatting: IO.SYS, MSDOS.SYS and COMMAND.COM. (In the case of original IBM PCs, the first two files are called IBMBIO.COM and IBMDOS.COM, respectively.) The /S option in the FORMAT command automatically copies these three system files when the tracks have been created.

If you request the directory of the formatted diskette, the list of files will contain only the COMMAND.COM file, the other two have been saved with the *hidden* attribute, due to which they are not visible in the directory. The CHKDSK command provides a complete view of the total capacity and the part of the disk used for the files (see section 4.6).

system diskette

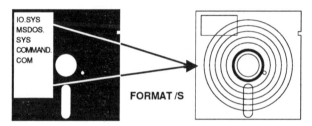

FORMAT /S

 In some MS-DOS versions, the /S option must be specified last.

The /V option, assigning a name to the diskette or harddisk. You can only keep a clear view of your diskettes if you attach labels to them with a title and/or concise summary. MS-DOS provides the possibility of registering the name on the diskette itself. You can allocate a (functional) name using the /V option in the FORMAT command. (This can also be done later using the LABEL command - see below in this section.)

When using the /V option, after the tracks have been formatted, the command will ask for a name of maximum 11 letters. Confirm the name by pressing Enter.

system diskette

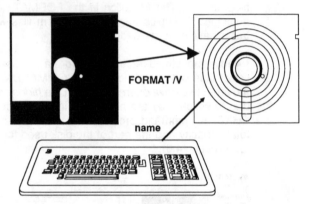

FORMAT /V

name

VOL, requesting the name of a diskette or harddisk.
The name of a diskette or harddisk is always stated during the implementation of the DIR instruction. You may also request the name separately.

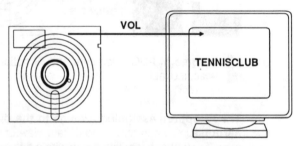

VOL

TENNISCLUB

The VOL instruction requests the name of the specified drive.

Command: Request the name of the storage medium (disk)

```
VOL d:
```

VOL = volume
d: = drive letter

Example 24: Format the diskette in drive B:. Copy the system files to this and assign a name to the diskette. The system diskette is in drive A:.

```
A:\>format  b:/u/s/u                     (1)
Insert new diskette for drive A:         (2)
and press ENTER when ready...

Formatting 360K
Format complete.
System transferred                       (3)

Volume label (11 characters, ENTER for none)? tennisclub   (4)

    362496 bytes total disk space
    119888 bytes used by system          (5)
    242688 bytes available on disk

      1024 bytes in each allocation unit.
       237 allocation units available on disk.

Volume Serial Number is 1348-17E2

Format another (Y/N)?n                   (6)


A:\>

C:\HSG>
```

(1) A format command along with the unconditional format option (U), the system files copy option (/S) and name allocation (/V).
(2) Statement similar to that in example 23.
(3) The program states that the three system files have been copied.
(4) The prompt for a name of maximum 11 characters for the diskette/harddisk. In the example, the diskette is to be used for the tennis club records. It makes no difference whether you type small or capital letters - MS-DOS always saves the name in capitals. The name may also contain numbers. Confirm the name by pressing Enter. If, after all, you do not wish to assign a name, press only Enter.

(5) The format program registers the capacity occupied
by the system files (in bytes).
(6) Dialogue as in example 23.

Example 25: Requesting details concerning the formatted diskette

```
A:\>dir a:                              (1)

 Volume in drive A is TENNISCLUB        (2)
 Volume Serial Number is 1348-17E2
 Directory of A:\

COMMAND  COM     47845 09/04/91    5:00  (3)
        1 file(s)      47845 bytes
                      242688 bytes free

A:\>vol a:                              (4)

 Volume in drive A is TENNISCLUB        (5)
 Volume Serial Number is 1348-17E2

A:\>
```

(1) Displays the directory of the specified drive. It is not
necessary, in this case, to specify the drive because
this already is the current drive.
(2) The name of the diskette.
(3) The list of files only contains COMMAND.COM,
which occupies 47,845 bytes. The previous example
shows that the system files occupy a total of 119,808
bytes, which means that 119,808-47,845 = 71,963
bytes are required for the two hidden files.
(4) Requests the name of A:.
(5) The name, and return to the prompt.

**Copying the system files to a diskette or harddisk
later.** If, during formatting, you have forgotten to copy
the system files to a diskette by using the /S option, this
can nevertheless still be done, but only on condition that
nothing has yet been saved on the diskette.

If you apply the SYS command to a used diskette, you
will always receive an error message, even if you have
deleted all files previously. During deletion, the file
names are rendered invisible to the directory, but the in-

formation remains on the diskette. This is useful if you wish to make files which have been accidentally deleted legible again using a special utility program, but in this case, the deleted files form an obstruction. The system files IO.SYS and MSDOS.SYS must be located on the first track of a diskette.

The SYS instruction only copies the IO.SYS and MSDOS.SYS files. COMMAND.COM and (if necessary) other system programs should be copied using COPY (see section 4.4). The position of these files on the diskette is unimportant.

system diskette

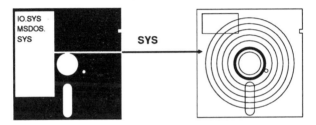

The instruction activates an *external system program* - place the system diskette in the current drive.

The SYS command copies hidden system files to a blank formatted diskette.

Command: Copy system files

```
SYS d:
```

SYS = system
d: = drive letter

Assigning a name to a diskette or harddisk later.
From MS-DOS version 3.0 onwards, it is possible to assign a name to a diskette or harddisk later, or to alter an existing name. The instruction activates an *external*

system program - place the system diskette in the current drive.

The LABEL instruction assigns a name to the specified diskette or harddisk.

Command: Assign a name to a diskette/harddisk

```
LABEL d:
```

LABEL = name
d: = drive letter

Example 26: Copy the most important system files to an empty, formatted diskette. The system diskette is located in drive A:, the empty diskette in drive B:.

```
A:\>sys b:                                      <1>
System transferred

A:\>copy \command.com b:                        <2>
        1 file(s) copied

A:\>label b:                                    <3>
Volume in drive B has no label
Volume Serial Number is 1348-17E2
Volume label (11 characters, ENTER for none)? tennisclub  <4>

A:\>dir b:                                      <5>

 Volume in drive B is TENNISCLUB                <6>
 Volume Serial Number is 1348-17E2
 Directory of B:\

COMMAND  COM     47845 09/04/91    5:00
        1 file(s)       47845 bytes
                       242688 bytes free

A:\>
```

(1) Copy the two hidden system files in A: to the empty, formatted diskette in B:. The program states that the command has been executed.
(2) Copy COMMAND.COM to the new diskette (see section 4.4).
(3) Assign a name to the new diskette (if the diskette already has a name, this will be shown as in the case of VOL).

(4) Type the name, see example 24.
(5) Display the directory of the new diskette.
(6) The specifications of the new diskette, analogous to example 25.

Example 27: The most common error messages when using FORMAT

```
A:\>format a:
Insert new diskette for drive A:
and press ENTER when ready...

Formatting 360K


Not ready                                        (1)
Format terminated.

Write protect error                              (2)

Invalid media or Track 0 bad - disk unusable     (3)

Invalid drive specification                      (4)

No room for system on destination disk           (5)

Invalid characters in volume label               (6)
```

(1) Error: Drive not ready
Remedy: (Place diskette and) close drive.
(2) Error: The diskette to be formatted is write-pro-
tected.
Remedy: Remove tape (5.25 inch) or close sleeve (3.5 inch).
(3) Error: It is not possible to copy the system files due to faulty disk.
Remedy: Repeat command using new diskette - per-
haps the old diskette can still be used to save information (not as start diskette).
(4) Error: Formatting not possible.
Remedy: Specify the proper drive, ensure that the parameters are valid for the specified drive. Perhaps the drive is defective.
(5) Error: Attempted to copy the system files to a used diskette using SYS.
Remedy: Format this diskette again.

(6) Error: Invalid characters specified in the file name.
Remedy: Assign a new file name.

4.4   Copying files

system diskette

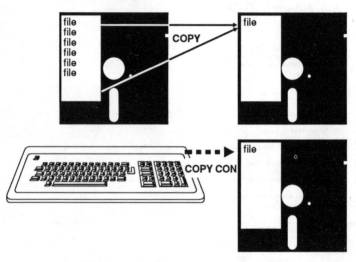

The copy command COPY enables you to:

■ copy individual files, groups of files or all files from
  one diskette to another
■ copy files from a diskette to a harddisk or vice versa,
  or from one harddisk to another
■ copy files from one directory to another on a harddisk
  (see section 7.2)
■ transport data between two peripheral devices or data
  from a diskette to a peripheral device or vice versa - for
  example, from the keyboard to a file on a diskette
■ gather the dispersed blocks of a fragmented file into
  a compact file, in order to increase the working speed
■ create backups of files by saving them once more
  under a different name
■ gather odd files into a single file.

The target diskette must be formatted.
The target diskette must have sufficient capacity for the files to be copied.
A file may only occur once on a diskette under a certain name (unless you make use of different directories).
If you copy a file of a certain name to a diskette containing a file of the same name, the file on the target disk will be overwritten without warning. Essential information may be lost!
If you are not sure, first request the directory in order to check if a certain name is already in use on the target diskette.
(The above-mentioned remarks also apply to the harddisk.)

The copy command activates an *internal system program* - the system diskette is not needed.
Specify the names of the source file and the target file in the command. If the copy is to have the same name as the original, it is not necessary to specify the target file. The way in which the names are specified influences the target direction. The ? and * wildcards may be used in the copy command.

The COPY command copies files between diskettes, harddisks and other devices.

Command: Copy files

```
COPY [d1:]file1.ext [d2:][file2.ext]
     [/A] [/B] [/V]
```

d1:   = letter of the source drive
d2:   = letter of the target drive

Special options:
/A   = (ASCII) - copy files in ASCII format: until the first end-of-file character (^Z, Ctrl+Z).

/B   = (BINARY) - copy files in binary format: until the real end of the file.

/V   = (VERIFY) - compare the copy to the source file.

Example 28: Copying individual files with A: as current drive

```
A:\>copy a:comm1.dat b:comm1.dat          (1)

A:\>copy comm1.dat b:                      (2)

A:\>copy a:comm1.dat b:nota.123            (3)

A:\>copy b:inter.92 a:inter.92             (4)

A:\>copy b:inter.92                        (5)

A:\>copy calculat.a16 price.a16            (6)

A:\>copy statist.186 statist.186           (7)

A:\>copy import.dat b:/v                   (8)
```

(1) The COMM1.DAT file is copied from the source diskette in drive A: to the target diskette in drive B:, under the same name.
Keep in mind the space between the command and the two file names.

(2) As in (1), but written more simply. If you do not specify a source drive, the command automatically applies to the current drive. It is always necessary to specify the target drive if this differs from the current drive. You may omit the second file name if the name of the copy is the same as the name of the original.

(3) The COMM1.DAT file on the diskette in drive A: is to be copied to drive B: under the name NOTA.123

(4) The INTER.92 file on the diskette in drive B: is to be copied to the current diskette under the same name.

(5) As in (4), but without explicitly naming the target drive because that is the current drive. The name of the copy is superfluous because it is not new.

(6) The command creates a copy of the CALCU-LAT.A16 file under the new name of PRICE.A16 on the same diskette in drive A:. When the process is com-

pleted, the diskette will contain two identical files with different names. You can work with one file and retain the other as backup.

(7) This command results in an error message because a file may not occur twice on the same diskette (in the same directory) under the same name.

(8) A copy is created of the IMPORT.DAT file from the diskette in drive A: on a diskette in drive B:. The /V option specifies that the copy program copies a sector and then compares the copy to the original. This somewhat retards the execution of the command.

Example 29: Copying groups of files

```
A:\>copy a:*.txt b:                       (1)

A:\>copy practice.* b:                     (2)

A:\>copy letter*.* b:                      (3)

A:\>copy copy ???guide.dat b:???value.dat  (4)

A:\>copy b:*.* a:                          (5)

A:\>copy a:*.* b:                          (6)

A:\>copy *.* b:                            (7)

A:\>copy c*.com b:                         (8)

B:\>copy *.bas c:*.txt                     (9)
```

With the exception of the last example, A: is the current drive.

(1) A copy is made on the diskette in drive B: of all the files on the diskette in drive A: which have the extension .TXT.

(2) As in (1), but now all files of the name PRACTICE with any extension.

(3) As in (1), but now all files whose names begin with LETTER.

(4) As in (1), but now for all files whose names begin with any three characters and end with GUIDE plus the extension .DAT. The copies of these files are saved under names with the same three characters at the beginning and end with VALUE.XYZ.

(5) Copies all files on the diskette in drive B: to the diskette in drive A:.
(6) As in (5), but now from drive A: to B:.
(7) As in (6), but written more shortly.
(8) Copies all files with the extension .COM (programs which are executable) from the harddisk to the diskette in drive B:.
(9) Copies all files with the extension .BAS (BASIC programs) from the diskette in drive B: to the harddisk C: and gives them the new extension .TXT (text file).

Example 30: Merging files

```
A:\>copy a:part1.txt+b:part2.txt c:total.txt   (1)

A:\>copy address.prg+adr.prg                   (2)

A:\>copy *.txt total.tex                        (3)

A:\>copy total.txt+*.txt                        (4)

A:\>copy *.tx1+*.tx2 total.tex                  (5)

A:\>copy value.com/b+calc.com answer.com        (6)
```

(1) Merges PART1.TXT on the diskette in drive A: with PART2.TXT on the diskette in drive B: to make the TOTAL.TXT file on the harddisk.
If the /B option is not specified, the contents of the files are combined as characters (ASCII format). Accordingly, text files can be merged in a simple manner.
The command is implemented if at least one of the specified files is present.
(2) The contents of the ADDRESS.PRG and ADR.PRG files on the diskette in drive A: are merged under the name of the file first mentioned in the current drive.

If you do not specify a target file, the second and all subsequent files will be added to the file first mentioned.
(3) Combines all files with the extension .TXT on the diskette in drive A: to one single file under the name TOTAL.TEX on the same diskette.
(4) The TOTAL.TXT file and all other files with the ex-

tension .TXT are combined in a new version of TOTAL.TXT. The difference with examples (3) and (4) is that in the first case, the combined file has a new name, while in the second case, the combined file has the name of the first original file which is, in fact, lost. The command attempts to copy TOTAL.TXT onto itself, which produces the ('error') message: 'Content of destination lost before copying'.

(5) Combines two groups of files into one file.

(6) The two files which can be implemented, VALUE.COM and CALC.COM are combined, using the binary option, into the file ANSWER.COM. The /B option also applies to all subsequent files, until something else is specified.

The /B option ensures that the files are entirely copied - thus not only up to a random end-of-file character (^Z) somewhere in the middle of a file.

Example 31: Copying text directly from the keyboard to a file. Combining two files and showing the result on the screen.

```
B:\>copy con part1.txt                                    (1)
This text has come directly from the keyboard.
It is only necessary to to press Enter if a sentence has to begin on a new line.
^Z
        1 file(s) copied

B:\>copy con part2.txt                                    (2)
The PART1.TXT text is concluded using Ctrl+Z or F6. After pressing Enter, the fi
le will be written to the current drive under the specified name.^Z
        1 file(s) copied

B:\>copy part1.txt+part2.txt total.txt                    (3)

PART1.TXT
PART2.TXT
        1 file(s) copied

B:\>type total.txt                                        (4)
This text has come directly from the keyboard.
It is only necessary to to press Enter if a sentence has to begin on a new line.


The PART1.TXT text is concluded using Ctrl+Z or F6. After pressing Enter, the fi
le will be written to the current drive under the specified name.
B:\>
```

In this example, we shall copy characters directly from a device to a file. The CON: (console) device is made up of two components: the keyboard for the input and the screen for the output.

(1) The command copies the text which has been entered from the memory to a file as soon as you confirm the end-of-file character by pressing Enter.
Due to the fact that ^Z is located on a new line, the combined file contains a blank line.
(2) As in (1), but now without new lines, even in the case of ^Z. The entire text is saved as one long line.
(3) The PART1.TXT and PART2.TXT files are saved on the current diskette under the name TOTAL.TXT.
Due to the fact that only one file is being written, the statement is probably different to what you expected.
(4) Displays the contents of TOTAL.TXT on the screen. Lines of more than 80 characters continue on the following line.

Example 32: The most common error messages concerning COPY

```
A:\>copy a:binker.txt b:                    (1)

Not ready reading drive A
Abort, Retry, Fail?a

A:\>copy a:binker.xtx alpha.txt             (2)
File not found - A:BINKER.XTX
        0 file(s) copied

A:\>copy a:binker.txt b:                     (3)
Insufficient disk space
        0 file(s) copied

A:\>copy binker.txt binker.txt              (4)
File cannot be copied onto itself
        0 file(s) copied

A:\>
```

(1) Error: There is no diskette in drive A:, or the drive is not locked.
Remedy: Place diskette in the drive and/or lock the drive.
(2) Error: The file specified is not on the diskette - perhaps this is a typing error.

Remedy: Request the list of files using DIR to search for the proper name.

(3) Error: There is not sufficient capacity on the diskette for the specified file.

Remedy: Use another diskette or delete the files you no longer need.

(4) Error: The command attempts to save a file under the same name again.

Remedy: Allocate another name to the copy.

4.5 Comparing copied files

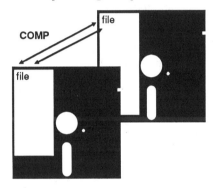

The COMP instruction enables you to:

■ Compare a copy of a file with the original on the same or another diskette or on harddisk.

■ Compare groups of files or all files as in the previous point.

■ Display the position of the differing data and display the differences themselves.

It is advisable to use the COMP instruction if you wish to be absolutely sure that the copies of files are identical to the originals. The DISKCOMP instruction does exactly the same with copies of complete diskettes which are made using DISKCOPY (see section 4.2).

The program which activates the COMP instruction

compares the original file to the copy, character by
character (bytes). If deviation is found, the program displays the following information:

■ The position, counted from 0, where the differing
   characters are located in the files (OFFSET).
■ The character in the file first specified and the character in the second file.

The compare program continues registering differences
to a maximum of 10 positions. If there are more differences, the progam gives a message to this effect and interrupts the comparison. It is then not worth the effort of
correcting the differences - making a new copy can be
done much more quickly.
The instruction activates an *external system program* -
the system diskette is needed.

**The COMP instruction compares files and registers
the deviations.**

Command: Compare files

```
COMP [d1:]file1.ext [d2:]file2.ext
```

COMP   = compare
d1:   = drive letter of the first diskdrive
d2:   = drive letter of the second diskdrive
file1.ext   = the original file
file2.ext   = the file to be compared

Example 33: Comparison of two files which have been
saved on different diskettes. Each diskette is located in
its own drive. (See diagram following page)

(1) Compare TESTFLE1.TXT to TESTFLE3.TXT on the
diskettes in the specified drives.
(2) The program states that the files are being compared.
(3) One file is longer than the other - the comparison is
discontinued.

```
A:\>comp a:testfle1.txt b:testfle3.txt      (1)
Comparing A:TESTFLE1.TXT and B:TESTFLE3.TXT...  (2)
Files are different sizes                   (3)

Compare more files (Y/N) ? y                (4)
Name of first file to compare: testfle1.txt (5)
Name of second file to compare: b:testfle2.txt
Option :
Comparing TESTFLE1.TXT and B:TESTFLE2.TXT...
Files compare OK                            (6)

Compare more files (Y/N) ? n                (7)

A:\>
```

(4) The program asks if you wish to compare other files. In the example we have answered Y (Yes).

(5) Specify the new file names: TESTFLE1.TXT and TESTFLE2.TXT.

(6) The files are identical.

(7) As in (4), answer N.

Example 34: Compare two files which are located on the harddisk under different names. The only difference lies in the last letters, 'e' and 'f', respectively.

```
C:\>type t1.txt                             (1)
billy binkerhill

C:\>type t2.txt                             (2)
billy binkerhilk

C:\>comp t1.txt t2.txt                       (3)
Comparing T1.TXT and T2.TXT...
Compare error at OFFSET F                    (4)
file1 = 6C                                   (5)
file2 = 6B                                   (6)

Compare more files (Y/N) ? n                 (7)

C:\>
```

(1) (2) Display the contents of the T1.TXT and T2.TXT files.

(3) Comparison instruction, analogous to example 33.

(4) Registration of a difference at hexadecimal position F, which is decimal position 15 (see information below). The program begins counting at zero - the *sixteenth* character differs.

(5) The deviating character 'I' in the first file has the ASCII code 6C hexadecimal, which is 108 in the decimal system.

(6) The deviating character 'k' in the second file has the ASCII code 6B hexadecimal, which is 107 decimally.

(7) Statement, analogous to example 33.

In some MS-DOS versions, COMP has the name FILECOMP or FC. The last two system programs are more extensive than COMP - they are more geared to computer programmers than to consumers.

Hexadecimal numbers are closer to the internal processing of data (computer language) than decimal numbers. Computer programmers can, for instance, represent the contents of the computer memory in the form of hexadecimal numbers.

In the hexadecimal (base 16) numeric system, sixteen different characters 01..89ABCDEF can be placed at each position of a number. The first position represents values from 0 to 15, the second position multiples of 16, the third position multiples of 256 (16x16) etc.

Examples:

hexadecimal	calculation	decimal
12	1x16+2x1	18
66	6x16+6x1	102
A7F	10x256+7x16+15x1	2687

The A is the eleventh and F is the sixteenth number in the hexadecimal numeric system (0 is the first number).

4.6 Checking the diskette or harddisk

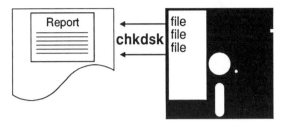

The contents of a diskette may be damaged as a result of various circumstances: careless treatment, wear and tear, the effects of a program etc. We wish to emphasize once again that it is extremely important to make at least one backup of each essential diskette.

If you suspect that a diskette contains errors, or even if you just wish to know how the contents of a diskette are divided, you can allow the diskette to be inspected by an MS-DOS system program. This program also contains an option which tracks down the faults and corrects them to a certain extent. (The information here concerning diskettes also refers to the harddisk.)
The program can implement the following procedures:

■ Check a diskette for errors in the directory and in the FAT (file allocation table).
■ Display statements concerning errors on the screen.
■ Correct simple errors.
■ Give a summary of the names and the size of all files (including hidden files) on the diskette.
■ Calculate the available capacity on the diskette.
■ Calculate the total and the available capacities of the computer memory.

The program does not examine the state of the files on the data section of the diskette (MS-DOS cannot be expected to know what should be there). If it appears that information has been damaged, you can try to restore it by using the RECOVER command (see section 4.7).

The system program checks if the directions in the directory conform to the (fragmented) chains of file clusters in the data section of the diskette. All information which is found during this check is displayed on the screen along with information concerning the computer. (You can interrupt the display by pressing Ctrl+Num-Lock and the transport of data to the printer by pressing Ctrl+PrintScreen.)

You can determine the intensity of this inspection by using various command options, which have a bearing upon the length of the report. The options deal with:

- The names of some or all files and the directory levels over which these are divided (see section 7.2).
- A list of information concerning incorrect directions in the directory or the FAT with reference to data clusters - for instance, loose clusters which are no longer part of a cluster chain in a file.
- The total storage capacity (bytes) of the diskette and the part of this in use for files and the part still available.
- The total capacity of the computer memory and the part of this still available.
- The amount of clusters on the diskette where (parts of) files are stored.

The CHKDSK instruction activates an *external system program* - the system diskette is needed.

The CHKDSK instruction inspects a diskette or harddisk for errors and corrects these if possible. The program displays a report which includes a list of all files and information concerning the total and available computer capacity.

Command: Check diskette/harddisk

```
CHKDSK [d:][file name] [/F] [/V]
```

CHKDSK   = check disk
d: = drive letter of the diskette/harddisk to
                  be inspected

file name   = name of one or more (all) files to be
                   inspected
/F   = (FIX) automatic correction of errors,
                   as much as possible
/V   = (VERIFY) displays the name of each
                   file checked

Example 35: Check the diskette in drive B:

```
A:\>chkdsk b:                                  (1)

Volume TENNISCLUB  created 15/09/1992 16:38    (2)
Volume Serial Number is 1348-17E2

    362496 bytes total disk space
     71680 bytes in 2 hidden files
     50176 bytes in 3 user files
    240640 bytes available on disk

      1024 bytes in each allocation unit
       354 total allocation units on disk
       235 available allocation units on disk

    655360 total bytes memory                  (3)
    487200 bytes free
```

(1) The system diskette is located in the current drive
(A:). Activate the command from this diskette. If your
computer only has one diskdrive, you must give the
command in this way too.
(2) The report firstly displays information concerning the
diskette: the name (if any), the date and time of formatting.
(3) The report contains further information concerning
the division of the storage capacity. The two hidden files
are: IO.SYS (IBMIO.COM) and MSDOS.SYS (IBM-
DOS.COM). In our case, these files occupy 71,680 characters (bytes). The three user files occupy 50,176 bytes.

Example 36: Check the harddisk C:, without automatic
correction of errors (see diagram following page)

(1) The command activates the check program from the
harddisk: if no letter is specified, the command refers to
C: (the harddisk).

```
C:\>chkdsk                                          (1)
Volume Serial Number is 184A-546C
Errors found, F parameter not specified             (2)
Corrections will not be written to disk


    1 lost allocation units found in 1 chains.      (3)
      2048 bytes disk space would be freed

 33449984 bytes total disk space                    (4)
   129024 bytes in 4 hidden files
    92160 bytes in 29 directories
 24872960 bytes in 1082 user files
  8353792 bytes available on disk

     2048 bytes in each allocation unit
    16333 total allocation units on disk
     4079 available allocation units on disk

   655360 total bytes memory                         (5)
   487200 bytes free

C:\>
```

(2) The program states that errors have been detected, but these will not be written on to the disk, since you have not specified the /F option (see example 37).

(3) The program registers that there is information on the disk which does not belong to any file.

(4) The statements are analogous to those in example 35, only now there are more hidden files. That may be a result of the fact that the system files are located in several places on the harddisk in different directories (see also section 7.1), or that an application has created hidden files.

(5) The computer memory, analogous to example 35.

Example 37: Check the harddisk, just as in the previous example, but now using the automatic correction function (see diagrams following page)

(1) The /F option makes corrections and creates files of these on the harddisk.

(2) The program asks if the loose clusters should be saved as files on the disk.

(3) Until now, the statements are identical to those in the previous example. The program registers the number of loose bytes taken up by (temporary) files.

```
C:\>chkdsk /f                              (1)
Volume Serial Number is 184A-546C

   1 lost allocation units found in 1 chains.  (2)
Convert lost chains to files (Y/N)?y

   33449984 bytes total disk space
     129024 bytes in 4 hidden files
      92160 bytes in 29 directories
   24872960 bytes in 1082 user files
       2048 bytes in 1 recovered files   (3)
    8353792 bytes available on disk

       2048 bytes in each allocation unit
      16333 total allocation units on disk
       4079 available allocation units on disk

     655360 total bytes memory
     487200 bytes free

C:\>
```

```
C:\>dir file*.*                            (4)

 Volume in drive C has no label
 Volume Serial Number is 184A-546C
 Directory of C:\

FILE0000 CHK      2048 16/09/92   11:24     (5)
         1 file(s)         2048 bytes
                        8353792 bytes free

C:\>
```

(4) The files created for the loose clusters which have been discovered receive the name FILExxxx.CHK automatically. In this, xxxx is an increasing number, beginning at 0000. In the example, the harddisk contains only one loose cluster - thus, the program creates only one file (FILE0000.CHK).
This command produces a selective list of the files with the recalled clusters.
(5) If you wish to know what these files contain, display them using the TYPE command. You can give a functional name to important information by using the REN(AME) option. Unimportant files can be deleted using DEL.

Example 38: Examine the diskette in drive A:, give a list of all files which have been examined and check if the files are stored in a contiguous (unified) manner on the diskette.

```
Volume TENNISCLUB  created 15/09/1992 16:38
Volume Serial Number is 1348-17E2
Directory A:\
A:\IO.SYS
A:\MSDOS.SYS
A:\COMMAND.COM
A:\TESTDAT1.TXT
A:\TESTDAT2.TXT

     362496 bytes total disk space
      71680 bytes in 2 hidden files
      50176 bytes in 3 user files
     240640 bytes available on disk

       1024 bytes in each allocation unit
        354 total allocation units on disk
        235 available allocation units on disk

     655360 total bytes memory
     487200 bytes free

All specified file(s) are contiguous

A:\>
```

(1) Activates the program from the harddisk. It is not actually necessary to specify drive A: as a parameter because this is also the current drive. The *.* file pattern ensures that the program checks all files. The /V option results in the program registering all files which have been checked, including the directories in which they are located.

(2) The program begins in the root directory. The standard name for this directory is \(backslash). This character is placed in front of all files which have been checked.

In the example, the contents of the diskette are not divided into (sub)directories: there are no other prefixes (paths) with the files. (We shall deal with the directory structure more extensively in section 7.2.)

(3) The CHKDSK instruction also checks the hidden files. Among other things, the diskette includes the system files for an IBM PC, IBMIO.COM and IBM-DOS.COM (instead of the IO.SYS and MSDOS.SYS for all other types of computers).

(4) This statement shows that the information blocks of all files are contiguous on the diskette.

4.7   Correcting defective files

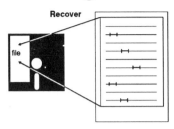

Imagine that the computer is loading a program from a diskette or that is is reading a data file. The following message is shown:

```
Data error reading drive A:
Abort, Retry, Fail?
```

Perhaps the reading problem will be solved if you press R (Retry). If the same message reappears, press A (Abort). This means that the current program will be discontinued. Start up the program again and see if reading is now possible.
In this section we shall discuss what you can do if the error message concerning the reading problem keeps returning.

Reading errors occur due to, among other things, information being incorrectly stored in the directory or in the data section of a disk, or due to damage to the data. If the FAT (file allocation table) on the diskette is still intact, it is usually possible to reconstruct the directions between the file blocks. The success of the recovery program depends on the extent of the damage.

Prevent problems, make frequent backups!

The MS-DOS RECOVER (utility) program deals with errors on a diskette in the following way:

■ Tracks down damaged sectors of a file and marks them.

■ Makes undamaged sectors accessible and combines them into a usable file.
■ Reconstructs a damaged directory and, accordingly, makes all files legible again.

The RECOVER program reads a file, sector by sector. Damaged sectors are marked and set aside (outside the sector chain of the file). At the end of the operation, the reconstructed file will probably have a different layout than the original file - not only have some sectors been cut away, the file will be stored in complete clusters of 1024 bytes again. The result may be that, at the end of the file, some unidentifiable characters, which did not appear in the original file, remain over. If the file contains text, you can then, using a word-processor, insert the lost passages, and delete the nonsense at the end.

It is almost always possible to make a disk legible again if the directory has been damaged. The pre-condition is that the file allocation table is still in order. The RE-COVERY correction program scrutinizes this table and assigns new names to all file registrations. These standard file names have the FILExxxx.REC pattern. In this, 'xxxx' is an increasing number, beginning at 0001. Loose clusters which remain over after applying RE-COVER can be made accessible using the CHKDSK command (see section 4.6).
Because RECOVER is an *external system program*, the system diskette is needed.

The RECOVER instruction reconstructs a file or makes all files on a diskette accessible again.

Command: Recover files

```
RECOVER [d:]file name
RECOVER d:
```

RECOVER   = recover, reconstruct
d: = letter of the drive containing the il-
               legible files
file name   = a specific file with an error

In the first version of the command, the program reconstructs only one file. The * and ? wildcards are allowed,
but they have no effect.
The second syntax applies to a diskette in which all files
have become inaccessible, owing to a damaged directory.

> Use the second syntax only if all other attempts to
> make the diskette legible again have failed (COPY
> to another disk and CHKDSK).
> If the directory of a harddisk is damaged, it is
> generally no longer possible to copy files. If you
> have backups of all files, the quickest method is to
> format the harddisk once more, create the directory
> structure again and copy the programs back again.
> In other cases, you will require assistance from an
> expert who will have to gather up the pieces using a
> special utility program.
>
> When the RECOVER program has been used, all
> files and directories have new names. Delete what
> you no longer need, allocate the original names to
> the files and correct the contents of the files.

Reconstructing one file

1 Make a copy of the file or of the whole diskette on
  another diskette.

2 Activate the RECOVER program (see examples 39
  and 40).

3 Display the contents of the reconstructed file using
  TYPE.

4 In the case of a text file or of another ASCII file, re-

place the missing parts and delete the superfluous characters.

5 If the reconstructed file is located on a diskette, copy all files to another diskette. Try to make the old disk-ette serviceable again by using the FORMAT in-struction. Discard the diskette if the command states that the diskette contains defective sectors.

Making a diskette or harddisk accessible when the directory has been damaged.

1 See if it is possible to display the directory using DIR. If this works, you can copy the files to another diskette using the COPY command. In order to copy an entire diskette, you can use the DISKCOPY com-mand.
   If the errors are located in one directory of the root directory, the files in the other directories will still be usable. First try CHKDSK on the directory containing the errors.

2 Activate the RECOVER program (see example 40). If the error is located in the directory of the harddisk, you cannot load RECOVER from the harddisk - use the system diskette.

3 Use CHKDSK to make loose blocks on the diskette accessible (see example 36).

4 Examine the new files using TYPE and check the contents.

5 Using COPY, copy the usable files under functional names to another diskette.

6 Format the harddisk when you have gathered all the files safely. The FORMAT command prevents the damaged sectors from being written upon.
   It is better not to use a diskette with defective sectors again. Dispense with it to save problems in the future.

7 Restore text files using a word-processor and copy them back to the harddisk, if required.

Example 39: Reconstruct the MSDOS04.TXT file on the diskette in drive A:.

```
A:\>c:recover msdos04.txt              (1)

Press any key to begin recovery of the    (2)
file(s) on drive A:


47845 of 47845 bytes recovered         (3)

A:\>dir                                (4)

 Volume in drive A is TENNISCLUB
 Volume Serial Number is 1348-17E2
 Directory of A:\

COMMAND  COM    47845 09/04/91    5:00
TESTDAT1 TXT       18 16/09/92   10:34
TESTDAT2 TXT       18 16/09/92   10:34
MSDOS04  TXT    47845 09/04/91    5:00     (5)
        4 file(s)     95726 bytes
                     192512 bytes free

A:\>
```

(1) Load the RECOVER program from the harddisk. Because drive A: is the current drive, it is not necessary to specify, along with the name of the file, that the file is located in drive A:.

(2) The program pauses to allow you the chance to load the diskette containing the damaged file - it will proceed when you press a random key.

(3) This statement means that the file has been reconstructed successfully.

(4) Display the directory.

(5) The file name is unchanged and the length of the file is unaltered since there are no defective sectors.

Example 40: Reconstruct all files on the diskette in drive A: (see diagram following page).

(1) Activate the program from the harddisk. Do not specify any files because the instruction is aimed at

making the entire diskette in the specified drive accessible again.

```
C:\>recover a:                              (1)
The entire drive will be reconstructed,
directory structures will be destroyed.
Are you sure (Y/N)? y
Press any key to begin recovery of the      (2)
file(s) on drive A:

6 file(s) recovered                         (3)

C:\HSG>dir a:                               (4)

 Volume in drive A has no label
 Volume Serial Number is 1348-17E2
 Directory of A:\

FILE0001 REC    33792 16/09/92   13:51     (5)
FILE0002 REC    37888 16/09/92   13:51
FILE0003 REC     1024 16/09/92   13:51
FILE0004 REC     1024 16/09/92   13:51
FILE0005 REC    48128 16/09/92   13:51
FILE0006 REC    48128 16/09/92   13:51
       6 file(s)     169984 bytes
                     192512 bytes free

C:\HSG>
```

(2) The same prompt as in example 39.
(3) The program registers the number of files it has reconstructed.
(4) Request the directory to view the names of the new
files.
(5) The date and time of the command to reconstruct
the files is shown adjacent to the files. You will observe
that the sizes of the files are all multiples of 1024 bytes
and that the original files have been deleted.

The root directory of a disk cannot contain an un-
limited amount of files. Due to the fact that all reconstructed files are placed in the root directory,
this may become overfull. The RECOVER program
is then discontinued and displays the message:

```
WARNING - directory full
```

Create space in the directory by copying to another
diskette, using COPY, those files which have already been reconstructed and files which are still
intact, and then delete them from the damaged

diskette using DEL. Start up the RECOVER program once more.

The recovered versions of files from branch directories are all saved in the root directory. The names of the directories are treated in the same way as files: the directories are also stored under the FILExxxx.REC name.

When you have recovered some or all of the files on a diskette, it is advisable not to use this diskette again. If the errors are a consequence of mechanical damage to the magnetic layer, reading errors can always recur. In the case of a harddisk, the defective sectors are rendered harmless by the FORMAT command, which jams these sectors.

The RECOVER command will not help in the case of badly damaged files or diskettes. If the files are indispensable, you can try to recover them using one of the special utility programs which are available in computer shops - for instance, PC Tools or Norton Utilities.

4.8 Changing the name of a file

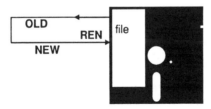

All kinds of circumstances occur which make it advisable to alter the name of a file:

- the contents of the file have been altered
- a new application of an unchanged file
- changing a default name, such as FILExxxx from CHKDSK or RECOVER, to a functional name.

We already know that it is possible to save a file under a new name on the same or on another diskette when using COPY. But if you use this method for a large amount of files, the original files still occupy disk capacity, and this makes the whole process rather inefficient if the diskette is too full to accommodate a copy of the file. This entails copying to another diskette, deleting the original file and copying the file back to the first diskette under a new name. If there is enough room on the diskette, an extra diskette will, of course, not be required, but the renaming process still requires two stages. In addition, the COPY command rewrites the file completely on the diskette and this is quite time-consuming.

MS-DOS has a special command which enables you to change the name of a file or a group of files directly. The RENAME instruction activates an *internal routine* - the system diskette is not needed.

The RENAME command changes the name of a file.

Command: Change the name of a file

```
RENAME [d:]oldfile.ext newfile.ext
[REN]
```

RENAME   = rename
REN   = abbreviated version of the command
d: = letter of the drive containing file to be
               renamed
oldfile.ext = old file name with extension
newfile.ext = new file name with (new) extension

The REN instruction does not make a copy - a drive letter in front of the new file name results in an error message and the command will not be implemented. Even if the original file is not located in the specified drive, the program will give an error message.

Many programs take specific names for their data files for granted. These programs jam or give an error message if you change the names of the files they use.

Example 41: Changing the name of the TESTFILE.TXT in drive A: to WORK.FLE

```
A:\>dir

 Volume in drive A has no label
 Volume Serial Number is 1348-17E2
 Directory of A:\

TESTFILE TXT         56 16/09/92   13:55
        1 file(s)            56 bytes
                        361472 bytes free

A:\>rename a:testfile.txt a:work.fle
Invalid parameter

A:\>rename a:testfile.txt work.fle
Duplicate file name or file not found

A:\>dir

 Volume in drive A has no label
 Volume Serial Number is 1348-17E2
 Directory of A:\

WORK     FLE         56 16/09/92   13:55
        1 file(s)            56 bytes
                        361472 bytes free
```

(1) Requests the directory of the diskette in drive A:.
(2) The command to change the name to A:WORK.FLE is invalid due to the drive specification. The program gives an error message.
(3) The correct way of writing the command. Because A: is the current drive, it is not necessary to specify this in front of the original file name.
(4) The new list of files shows that the name change has taken place correctly.

Example 42: An attempt to rename an absent file, and renaming groups of files (see diagram following page)

(1) The T1.TXT file is not located on the current diskette - the program gives an error message (....not found).

The program also gives an error message if the new name already exists on the current disk (...duplicate file).

```
A:\>rename t1.txt values.123              (1)
Duplicate file name or file not found

DATA      TXT       56 16/09/92   13:55   (2)
T2        TXT       11 16/09/92   14:02
          2 file(s)         67 bytes
                       360448 bytes free


A:\>rename *.txt *.dat                    (3)

DATA      DAT       56 16/09/92   13:55   (4)
T2        DAT       11 16/09/92   14:02
          2 file(s)         67 bytes
                       360448 bytes free


A:\>rename *.* *.txt                      (5)

DATA      TXT       56 16/09/92   13:55   (6)
T2        TXT       11 16/09/92   14:02
          2 file(s)         67 bytes
                       360448 bytes free
```

(2) The list of files on the diskette we are using in this example.
(3) All files retain their names - only those files with the extension .TXT have their extension altered to .DAT.
(4) The alteration of the extensions has taken place correctly.
(5) The names of the files remain unchanged, but all extensions are altered to .TXT.
(6) The file list after the extension changes.

4.9   Deleting a file

To save room on the disk, it is better to delete files which are no longer in use and files which are full of nonsense. Even if you are not planning to replace these with new files, a short file list has the advantage of being easy to refer to.

The instruction which we shall deal with in this section can be used to delete both individual files and groups of files. The instruction is not valid for hidden system files. If you wish to delete these, there is no other alternative, in the meantime, to formatting the diskette or harddisk.

Consider carefully before you delete one or more files. Using the MS-DOS commands, it is not possible to recover deleted files. The deletion program makes the file name untraceable by changing the first character of the name.
Your computer supplier has utility packages (Norton Utilities, PC Tools, DiskDoctor) which enable you, among other things, to make a deleted file visible again in the directory, i.e. to 'undelete' it.

MS-DOS contains two *internal instructions* to delete files; both have the same effect.

The DEL and ERASE instructions remove one or more files.

Command: Delete file

```
DEL [d:]file.ext
ERASE [d:]file.ext
```

DEL   = delete
ERASE   = erase
d: = drive with the diskette containing the file to be deleted
file.ext   = name of the file to be deleted

The ? and * wildcards may be used in file names in deletion commands.

Due to the fact that wildcards generally make a command valid for various files, there is a reasonable chance that a delete command containing wildcards will delete files which should be retained. Accordingly, prior to the delete command, you should give the 'DIR [d:]file.ext' command in order to observe the effect of the wildcards. Subsequently change the command using the command buffer: F1, E, L, F3. The result is 'DEL [d:]file.ext'.

The most drastic delete command is DEL *.*. MS-DOS will automatically respond with the question as to whether you are really sure. Reconsider before confirming.

The delete commands cannot delete a (sub)directory from the directory structure. To do this, the RMDIR instruction is necessary (see section 7.2).

From MS-DOS version 3.0 onwards, you can write-protect a file using the ATTRIB instruction. This concerns the Read Only attribute. Files with this attribute cannot be overwritten or deleted.

Example 43: Delete the LETTER0.TXT file on the diskette in drive A:.

```
A:\>dir

 Volume in drive A has no label
 Volume Serial Number is 1348-17E2
 Directory of A:\

LETTER0  TXT      2048 16/09/92   14:07
LETTER1  TXT      2064 16/09/92   14:07
LETTER2  TXT       932 16/09/92   14:07
        3 file(s)        5044 bytes
                       356352 bytes free

A:\>del letter0.txt

A:\>dir

 Volume in drive A has no label
 Volume Serial Number is 1348-17E2
 Directory of A:\

LETTER1  TXT      2064 16/09/92   14:07
LETTER2  TXT       932 16/09/92   14:07
        2 file(s)        2996 bytes
                       358400 bytes free
A:\>
```

(1) The list of files on the diskette in drive A:.

(2) In this case, the drive does not have to be specified in the command because drive A: is the current drive. If the file has an extension, it may not be omitted from the command (use the * wildcard if necessary).

(3) The list of files on the diskette in drive A: again.

(4) The LETTER0.TXT is no longer accessible. The 2048 bytes occupied by the file are available for use again - the number of bytes available on the diskette has risen from 356,352 to 358,400.

Example 44: Delete all files with the .SCR extension from the harddisk C:.

```
A:\>dir c:*.scr                              (1)

 Volume in drive C has no label
 Volume Serial Number is 184A-546C
 Directory of C:\

BILLY    SCR         8 16/09/92   14:13
BINKER   SCR         6 16/09/92   14:13
HILL     SCR        30 16/09/92   14:13
         3 file(s)          44 bytes
                     8347648 bytes free

A:\>del c:*.scr                              (2)

A:\>dir c:*.scr                              (3)

 Volume in drive C has no label
 Volume Serial Number is 184A-546C
 Directory of C:\

File not found                               (4)

A:\>
```

(1) Drive A: is the current drive. The command displays the list of all files on the harddisk C: which have the .SCR extension.

(2) The drive letter of the harddisk must be specified because A: is the current drive.

(3) Inspect the result of the delete command.

(4) The program registers that there is no (further) file conforming to the specified file pattern.

Example 45: Delete all files on the diskette in drive A:

```
A:\>dir                                  (1)

 Volume in drive A has no label
 Volume Serial Number is 1348-17E2
 Directory of A:\

LETTER1  TXT     2064 16/09/92   14:07
LETTER2  TXT      932 16/09/92   14:07
LETTER3  TXT      932 16/09/92   14:07
        3 file(s)       3928 bytes
                      357376 bytes free

A:\>erase *.*                            (2)
All files in directory will be deleted!
Are you sure (Y/N)?y                     (3)

A:\>dir
                                         (4)
 Volume in drive A has no label
 Volume Serial Number is 1348-17E2
 Directory of A:\

File not found                           (5)

A:\>
```

(1) The instruction displays the list of all files on the diskette in drive A:.
(2) For a change, we shall use the ERASE command.
The *.* file pattern represents all files except the hidden
system files.
(3) Only affirm if you are certain that all files should be
deleted. Answering N results in the program being discontinued and the system returning to the prompt A>.
(4) Checking the list of files once more.
(5) Because all files have been deleted, no file can be
found.

4.10   Exercises

1   Always make backups of all diskettes containing
    programs or information. Do this with the system
    diskette. Make a copy of the original diskette.

2   Compare the contents of the new system diskette to
    those of the original diskette.

3   Make another copy of the system diskette, but now
    using different instructions. Take another blank disk-

ette, format it and copy the hidden system files simultaneously. Assign the name SYSCOPY to the new
diskette.

4 Copy all external system programs from the original
   system diskette to the formatted new diskette.

5 Compare the files on the original system diskette to
   those on the copy. To reduce work, make the comparison collectively using *.COM, *.EXE, *.SYS and
   *.BAT.

6 Format another diskette, this time without system
   programs.

7 Check the state of the formatted empty diskette. Use
   another diskette for the remainder of the exercise if
   the report shows faults.

8 Place the hidden system files on the empty diskette.
   Make a new report concerning the diskette and
   examine the available capacity. Accordingly, you
   can work out the capacity occupied by the hidden
   system files.

9 Copy the DISKCOPY external system program from
   the original system diskette to the new diskette
   under the name COPY.COM and check the result by
   requesting the list of files on the new diskette. Re-
   allocate the original name to the copy program on
   the new diskette.

10 Delete DISKCOPY.COM from the new diskette and
   then copy all system programs to the new diskette
   using wildcards. Check the result by examining the
   list of files on the new diskette.

5   Batch files

5.1   Operation and application of batch files

Many processes which use the operating system require a fixed series of instructions. If, for instance, you make a copy of a diskette and then wish to view the contents of the copy, the following two instructions are necessary:

Copy command   DISKCOPY A: B:
Display list of files   DIR B:

MS-DOS provides the possibility of combining one or more instructions into a package which can be activated and then implemented by the operating system. A package like this is called a *batch*. The instructions are stored in a text file with the extension 'BAT'. If you activate this file, the operating system reads the separate commands and executes these in the given order of sequence.

Batch files make working with your computer much easier. For example, they enable you to:

■ reduce the amount of typing work
■ limit the errors in input
■ use own names for instructions without changing the file names
■ allow system setups to be done automatically when the computer is started up
■ save new data automatically when a program is terminated.

The instructions for the computer are written to a file in the same order of sequence as you type them. The computer implements the batch file as follows:

■ The operating system reads an instruction in the batch file.

- The computer executes the instruction.
- The operating system returns to the batch file and continues with the next instruction, until all commands have been implemented.

The .BAT extension is reserved for batch files.

5.2 Starting up a batch file

Start up a batch file by specifying the name.

Command: Start up a batch file

```
[d:]file[.BAT]
```

d: = drive letter of the diskette containing the batch file.
        If you do not specify a drive letter, the operating system will search for the batch file on the current drive.
file   = the name of the batch file
.BAT   = the standard extension, which you do not need to enter.

Example:
The COPY.BAT file contains the following instructions:

```
DISKCOPY A: B:
DIR B:
```

Activate the batch file by typing 'COPY' and pressing Enter. The operating system will automatically execute both commands in the specified order of sequence.

5.3 Creating a batch file

A batch file can be created using practically any word-processor. The only condition is that the text file may not contain any formatting codes from the word-processor, but that is not a problem for most word-processors. In order to create a batch file, you can use, for instance, the EDLIN line editor which is mostly located on the MS-DOS system diskette.

Because most batch files are quite short, the COPY CON command is an efficient alternative (see section 4.4).

The COPY CON instruction enables you to write a text from the keyboard directly to a file (text file, ASCII format). The disadvantage of this method is that you can only alter a line as long as you have not yet pressed Enter in order to move on to the next instruction. If you subsequently discover an error, you have to type the whole file again, which is not disastrous since the size of the file is never very large. Nevertheless, it is advisable to work out the commands on paper first. (Of course, you can always load the batch file into your word-processor and rectify the error there.) The example below illustrates the COPY CON process.

Example 46: Write the CCOPY.BAT batch file (see sections 5.1 and 5.2) and implement it

```
C:\>copy con ccopy.bat                    (1)
diskcopy a: b:
dir b:
^Z
        1 file(s) copied                  (2)

C:\>ccopy                                 (3)

C:\>diskcopy a: b:                        (4)

Insert SOURCE diskette in drive A:        (5)

Insert TARGET diskette in drive B:

Press any key to continue . . .
^C                                        (6)

C:\>dir b:                                (7)

 Volume in drive B has no label
 Volume Serial Number is 3A60-16D6
 Directory of B:\

File not found                            (8)
```

(1) The harddisk is the current drive. The COPY CON instruction copies the keyboard input to the CCOPY.BAT file. Place each instruction on a separate line and complete each line by pressing Enter. The batch file consists of only two commands.

(2) The F6 function key places an end-of-file mark. Instead of F6, you can also press the Ctrl+Z key combination. As soon as you indicate the end of the file by pressing Enter, it is written to the CCOPY.BAT file on the diskette in the current drive (to the harddisk C: in our example).

(3) Typing the name CCOPY is sufficient to implement the CCOPY.BAT batch file.

(4) The file is started up: the DISKCOPY instruction is activated automatically.

(5) The two statements of the DISKCOPY instruction are displayed successively, followed immediately by the prompt for any random key.

(6) It is not really our intention to make a copy of a diskette during this test. Discontinue the command by pressing the Ctrl+C key combination.

(7) The operating system continues with the next instruction in the batch file: requesting the list of files on the diskette in drive B:.

(8) Because nothing has been copied, the directory is empty and DIR displays a statement to this effect.

5.4 Instructions for batch files

You can not only use the normal DOS commands in batch files, you can also use instructions which are valid only for batch files.
There are special instructions for the following objectives:

■ Including commentary (information) in the file and displaying it on the screen.

■ Displaying or omitting statements from the operating system.

■ Interrupting the execution of the batch file, displaying a statement, and resuming the execution by pressing a random key.

■ By-passing the execution of a part of batch file or stopping the implementation completely.
■ Along with the activation of the batch file, the addition of various information which can be slotted into the commands in the batch file at a chosen place.
■ The operation of small programs.

We shall first deal with the batch instructions individually. We shall apply them in a logical combination in examples 47 and 48. (The operating instructions for batch programs lie outside the scope of this book. There is a summary of these in the appendix.)

The REM batch command places a remark in a batch file. The remark also appears on the screen, unless the system statements have been switched off.

Command: Place commentary in a batch file

```
REM [text]
```

REM = remark
text = chosen text (without apostrophes), max. 123 characters. In the case of no text, REM places an empty line in the batch file.

Example:

```
REM*** Start up the GWBASIC interpreter
automatically ***
```

This line will be automatically displayed by a batch file, if the system statements are switched on (see ECHO).

The ECHO batch instruction switches the display of the instructions and the commentary on and off.

Command: Switch the display of the instructions on and off

```
ECHO [ON/OFF/text]
```

ECHO = the instruction runs the current mode if no
        parameters are specified
ON   = display instructions
OFF   = no display, only execution of instructions
text = if the ON and OFF parameters are not
        specified, the instruction will display the
        'text', even if ECHO is set to the OFF
        mode.

Example:

```
ECHO OFF
ECHO Place a diskette in B: and lock the
diskdrive
```

A batch file with these lines displays the following on the screen:

```
A>ECHO OFF
Place a diskette in B: and lock the diskdrive
```

The first line switches off the display of the instructions: the text display appears *without* the word ECHO.

The PAUSE batch instruction interrupts the execution of a batch file, shows a statement if required, and continues the execution when you press a random key.

Command: Interrupt a batch process

```
PAUSE [text]
```

PAUSE = pause
text = chosen text (without apostrophes), max.
        121 characters. The text will not appear on
        the screen if ECHO is set to OFF.

Example:

```
PAUSE Place a diskette in drive B:
```

If this line is located in a batch file, the following will appear on the screen:

```
A>PAUSE Place a diskette in drive B:
Press any key ...
```

You can always stop the execution of a batch file by using the Ctrl+C or Ctrl+Break key combinations.

The operating system will ask whether you wish to terminate the batch file (Terminate batch program (Y/N)?). If you respond N, only the current instruction (or the activation of a program) will be discontinued.

Example 47: Create a batch file illustrating the REM, ECHO and PAUSE instructions and the discontinue function

```
C:\>copy con test3.bat                        (1)
echo off
echo Test the PAUSE instruction
pause This text does not appear on the screen
echo on
pause This text DOES appear on the screen
rem ****** End of the test ******
^Z
        1 file(s) copied                      (2)

C:\>test3                                      (3)

C:\>echo off                                   (4)
Test the PAUSE instruction                     (5)
Press any key to continue . . .                (6)
^C

Terminate batch job (Y/N)?n                    (7)

C:\>pause This text DOES appear on the screen  (8)
Press any key to continue . . .

C:\>rem ****** End of the test ******          (9)

C:\>
```

(1) The harddisk is the current drive. Assign the name TEST3.BAT to the batch file.

(2) End of file - press Enter to write the file to the hard-disk.

(3) Activate the batch file.

(4) Do not display instructions.

(5) The test is displayed via the ECHO instruction. The same text behind the REM instruction would not, in this case (ECHO OFF), be displayed.

(6) This text is shown on the screen by the *first* PAUSE instruction. These system statements have high priority - they are implemented despite the ECHO OFF mode. Accordingly, the text behind the first PAUSE instruction is not displayed.

The Ctrl+C key combination has been pressed here. This interrupts the current operating system process - 'Press a key....'.

(7) The operating system continues with the following command, which is also a system statement with high priority. Owing to the N response, the current command in the batch file is discontinued, but the operating system continues with the following command in the batch file.

(8) Because the ECHO mode is ON, the text behind the second PAUSE instruction is displayed on the screen. The operating system continues with the following command in the batch file when you press any key.

(9) Owing to ECHO ON, not only the instruction but also the text appears on the screen.

Behind the command to activate a batch file, you can also register parameters which can be specified in the commands in the batch file. You can register a maximum of *nine parameters* in each instruction. (We shall not discuss, at this stage, the possibility of extending this amount using the SHIFT instruction.) The variables have the codes %1 to %9 in the batch file. They may appear anywhere in the instruction. The tenth variable, %0, contains the name of the file itself. The name must be saved in order to be able to return to the file after another batch file has been activated.

**The following syntax enables you supply informa-
tion to the instructions in a batch file.**

Command: Enter information for a batch job.

```
name value1 value2 ...
```

name   = name of the batch file
value1   = value of a variable in the batch file;
              space as separation character

Example 48: Create a batch file, TEST, in order to
make, in an easy way, a backup copy of the diskette in
drive A:

```
A:\>copy con test.bat              (1)
copy a:%1 a:%2                     (2)
dir a:%2                           (3)
type a:%0.bat                      (4)
^Z
        1 file(s) copied           (5)

A:\>test data.txt values.123       (6)
A:\>copy a:data.txt a:values.123   (7)
        1 file(s) copied

A:\>dir a:values.123               (8)

 Volume in drive A has no label
 Volume Serial Number is 1348-17E2
 Directory of A:\

VALUES   123        8 16/09/92  16:16
        1 file(s)          8 bytes
                     359424 bytes free

A:\>type a:test.bat                (9)
copy a:%1 a:%2
dir a:%2
type a:%0.bat
```

(1) Create the TEST.BAT batch file.
(2) Copy command. The file represented by the name in
%1 is to be copied to a file represented by %2 on the
diskette in drive A:. The variables receive values when
activated as shown in point (6). The name of the batch
file is located in %0, the first parameter in %1, the second in %2 and so forth. An instruction can consist of a
maximum of ten elements including the name of the

batch file. These elements are separated by spaces. Specification of the drives is not necessary in this command because A: is the current drive.

(3) Display only the information of those files whose name corresponds to %2 in the file list. Accordingly, you can check if the command has been properly implemented - after copying, the copy is located on the diskette under the name which occurs in the %2 variable.

(4) Display the contents of the file whose name corresponds to the %0 variable - this is the batch file itself.

(5) Save the completed batch file on the diskette.

(6) Activate the TEST.BAT batch file (see point (2)). Here, the extension does not need to be specified. The name of the batch file is saved in %0, DATA.TXT in %1 and VALUES.123 in %2.

(7) The operating system executes the first command. The system statements show that the parameters have taken the place of the variables.

(8) Shows the registration of the copy in the directory (under the name VALUES.123).

(9) Displays the contents of the batch file.

5.5 Automatic start-up file, AUTOEXEC.BAT

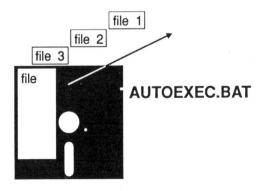

In chapter 1, we saw that the MS-DOS starting-up procedure consisted of four stages:

■ A computer self-test which is independent of the operating system.
■ Loading the most important system programs from the system diskette.
■ Searching for the start-up file, AUTOEXEC.BAT.
■ Loading and implementing the start-up file (if present).

The automatic start-up file may occur as an external system file on the system diskette, but that is not necessarily the case.
The start-up file assumes a number of jobs which you would otherwise have to do manually when starting up the computer - registering date and time, switching to the directory containing the word-processor, activating the word-processor etc. Due to the fact that these requirements differ according to the individual user, there are no standard contents regarding the start-up file. Perhaps there is already a start-up file on your system diskette - this can easily be checked because the name is always AUTOEXEC.BAT.

Example 49: Searching on the harddisk for AUTOEXEC.BAT and displaying its contents

```
C:\>dir autoexec.bat

 Volume in drive C has no label
 Volume Serial Number is 184A-546C
 Directory of C:\

AUTOEXEC BAT          27 16/09/92   16:24
        1 file(s)            27 bytes
                        8073216 bytes free

C:\>type autoexec.bat
echo off
cls
date
time

C:\>
```

(1) The harddisk is the current drive. This instruction shows the registration of the specified file in the directory.

(2) The start-up file is available - the information is displayed.

(3) Shows the contents of the start-up file on the screen.

(4) Switches off the system statements.

(5) Clears screen.

(6) Activates the internal system program to register date.

(7) Activates the internal system program to set the clock. The batch file waits in order to give you the chance to enter the date and time. Confirm both values by pressing Enter. These commands are superfluous if your computer has a clock which is powered by a battery. In this case, there is an instruction which adopts the information from the automatic calendar and clock (TIMER/I for instance) instead of the program.

You now have sufficient know-how to be able to create a start-up file personally. Just to be sure, give the original start-up file another name, or make a copy on a diskette. You can always rely on this if the new version does not work satisfactorily. Another safety measure, for instance, is to allocate an interim name to the new file, AUTO.BAT for example.

Using AUTOEXEC.BAT, you are able to activate the program which you mostly run: the word-processor, the calculator, the databank etc. when you start up the computer.

Example 50: The proposed start-up file should load and start up WordPerfect 5.0 automatically. The batch file should receive the interim name AUTO.BAT and, if found to be adequate, the definite name AUTOEXEC.BAT.

```
C:\>copy con auto.bat                              (1)
echo off                                           (2)
cls
graphics                                           (3)
date                                               (4)
time
cls
echo      Word-processing using WordPerfect 5.1    (5)
echo      Place the program diskette
echo           in diskdrive A:,
echo      and the work diskette
echo           in diskdrive B:.
echo      Lock both drives.
pause                                              (6)
wp                                                 (7)
^Z                                                 (8)

C:\>type auto.bat                                  (9)

C:\>rename auto.bat autoexec.bat                   (10)
```

(1) Create the AUTO.BAT batch file.

(2) Instructions analogous to example 49.

(3) If the GRAPHICS program is active, you can transport the current contents of the screen to the printer,
presuming that your computer has a colour graphics
adapter (see section 3.4).

(4) Instructions analogous to example 49.

(5) Display text lines.

(6) The PAUSE command provides the chance to read
the text before the program continues with the next
command in the batch file. The statement here reminds
you to place the diskettes containing the word-processor in the drives, otherwise the system will try to start up
WordPerfect before the program and the text files are
available. (The program will then give an error statement which can be avoided.)

(7) This command loads and starts up the WordPerfect
word-processor.

(8) Close the batch file and save it on the diskette. (To
save space, we shall not show this statement here.)

(9) Command to display the contents of the batch file on
the screen.

(10) Assign the standard name for a start-up file
(AUTOEXEC.BAT) to the AUTO.BAT file. If there is already a file called AUTOEXEC.BAT on the diskette, you
must first delete it using the 'DEL AUTOEXEC.BAT'
command.

In chapter 7, when dealing with the SELECT command, we shall discuss how to have MS-DOS create a start-up file itself. Many applications, using their installation procedures, are able to adjust an existing start-up file to the new situation.

5.6 Exercises

1 The 'FORMAT B:' and 'COPY *.* B:' commands are often used in conjunction, in order to write all files in a unified form to a new diskette. The 'DISKCOPY A:B:' command copies the files with the same fragmented structure as on the source diskette. Write a batch file with these two instructions.

2 As an experiment, create a new automatic start-up file, AUTOEXEC.BAT. Proceed as follows:

■ Place the system diskette in drive A:.
■ Check, using 'DIR *.BAT' if there is already a file with the name AUTOEXEC.BAT.
■ If required, make a backup of this file under the name HELP.BAT using the command 'COPY autoexec.bat help.bat'.
■ Delete the original file using 'DEL autoexec.bat'.
■ Create, using 'COPY CON ...' a new AUTOEXEC.BAT containing the following:

ECHO OFF   (system statements switched off)
GRAPHICS   (only in the case of a colour graphics adapter)
DATE   (enter current date)
TIME   (enter current time)
GWBASIC   (or another BASIC interpreter or another program which can be implemented

■ Check the contents of AUTOEXEC.BAT using the command 'TYPE autoexec.bat'.
■ Start up the computer again using the key combination for a warm boot: Ctrl+Alt+Del.
■ The computer should now proceed to the initial

BASIC screen (or that of another specified program).
■ Quit the BASIC interpreter using the SYSTEM command.
■ Restore the original situation by deleting the newly-made batch file using the 'DEL...' command. Allocate the standard name for a start-up file to the HELP.BAT file, using the instruction 'RENAME help.bat autoexec.bat'.

6   Adjusting the operating system

6.1   The configuration file CONFIG.SYS

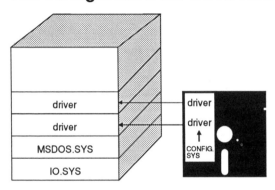

It is desirable to adjust the operating system as precisely as possible to the specific combination of devices in and around your computer. Perhaps you are using a cassette recorder as background memory, or a printer and a keyboard which are not compatible with MS-DOS norms. It may also occur that a program with which you are working requires a special memory setup (buffers, extensions).

In these cases, *drivers* are necessary for the proper link between device and operating system. Normally, there are several drivers on the system diskette - you only need to activate them. If you acquire a new peripheral device, a corresponding driver is generally supplied along with it. Copy this driver to your system diskette. Nevertheless, there is a good chance that you will require the assistance of your supplier to find the correct parameters for your specific hardware combination. If you possess all the technical specifications and you are experienced in programming in ASSEMBLER, you can create a driver yourself.

MS-DOS has a special file where the instructions for the drivers and their parameters are located. This has the advantage that the configuration is automatically set up in the correct manner when the computer is started up. (A configuration is the combination of linked components in the computer.) This file has the compulsory name CONFIG.SYS.

> You are not obliged to use a configuration system. In its absence, the operating system works using defaults.
> Ensure that programs which are summoned using CONFIG.SYS are available at the specified place on the system disk. Otherwise, the operating system will not be able to locate them when starting up and you will receive an error statement.

6.2   Composing or altering CONFIG.SYS

The configuration file is a text file (ASCII format). With respect to the operating system, it fulfils the function of a permanent external memory for commands and program names.

A configuration file is generally not very long, so that, just as in the case of the starting-up file, it can be written using the COPY CON command. Examine whether a CONFIG.SYS file is present on the system diskette or harddisk, and, if so, inspect the contents. Protect this file by assigning it another name or by making a copy on another diskette. Assign a neutral name to the new file in the meantime, and rename it CONFIG.SYS when you have corrected any erroneous elements in the content.

Example 51: Check if the diskette in drive A: contains a file with the name CONFIG.SYS. Display the contents on the screen and write a new configuration file under the name CONTEST.BAT.

```
A:\>dir config.sys                    (1)

 Volume in drive A has no label
 Volume Serial Number is 1348-17E2
 Directory of A:\

CONFIG    SYS        8 16/09/92  16:32  (2)
         1 file(s)        8 bytes
                   358400 bytes free

A:\>type config.sys                   (3)
break on                              (4)
A:\>copy con contest.bat              (5)
break on                              (6)
buffers=15
files=20
^Z                                    (7)
         1 file(s) copied

A:\>type contest.bat                  (8)

A:\>del config.sys                    (9)

A:\>ren contest.bat config.sys        (10)
```

(1) Search for the CONFIG.SYS file.
(2) The system has located the file.
(3) Show the contents on the screen.
(4) The file contains only one instruction (see section 6.3).
(5) Create a new file with the name CONTEST.BAT.
(6) For more information concerning these commands we refer you to section 6.3.
(7) Save the completed file.
(8) Show the contents of the file on the screen (not shown in the diagram).
(9) Delete the original configuration file.
(10) Assign the standard name CONFIG.SYS to the file.

6.3 The most important commands in CONFIG.SYS

Most computer users appear to deploy only a few of the instructions which are available to a configuration file. Of the instructions which were available prior to MS-DOS version 3.0, we shall deal with DEVICE, BUF-FERS, FILES and BREAK because many applications expect a setup using these. From version 2.11 on-

wards, the COUNTRY instruction is of some import-
ance. We shall discuss the SHELL and LASTDRIVE instructions briefly and without examples. We shall ignore
FCBS completely because comprehension of this requires extensive knowledge of the operating system. All
these instructions activate internal system programs -
the system diskette is not needed.

Adjustment to non-standard devices. The IO.SYS
(IBMBIO.COM), MSDOS.SYS (IBMDOS.COM) system
programs contain routines which regulate the exchange of
data between the computer and the standard peripheral
devices: diskdrives, harddisks, screens and keyboards. If
you connect a device which is not compatible with the
standard software, you will require a special driver.

**The DEVICE instruction installs a driver for a device
via the CONFIG.SYS file.**

Command: Activate a driver for a device

```
DEVICE=driver
```

DEVICE   = device
driver   = driver from the manufacturer, or your
            own

Many applications demand a more extensive operation
of the keyboard and screen than the standard possibilities provide. The MS-DOS package provides the
ANSI driver for objectives like these. Check if this file is
located on your system diskette, and if so, install it using
CONFIG.SYS.

Example:
Install the driver for the screen and keyboard

Procedure: Write the following instruction in CON-
FIG.SYS:

```
DEVICE=ANSI.SYS
```

Reserve blocks in memory. The exchange of data between computer and the storage media takes place using areas in the computer memory. Normally, a number of blocks (buffers) of 512 bytes is reserved for interim storage when reading and writing. The contents of an entire number of blocks fits into a sector on the disk. The operating system collects data until the sector is full and then writes them to the disk in one go.

Using MS-DOS, you can choose the number of buffers between 1 and 99. Each buffer occupies 528 bytes of memory (16 bytes for management). Accordingly, a large number of buffers entails less memory for programs etc.

The larger the memory, the more capacity there is for buffers, but both a very small and a very large number of buffers have disadvantages with respect to reading and writing speeds. The type of program determines whether many or few (and often or seldom) pieces of information are transported between computer and disk. A database program reads and writes a great deal - it requires relatively many buffer blocks. Pure calculation programs (spreadsheets) make much less demand upon background memory.
Normally, MS-DOS works with two buffers, but in the case of a harddisk, at least three are necessary.

The BUFFERS instruction installs the number of disk buffers for the operating system.

Command: Install disk buffers

```
BUFFERS=x
```

BUFFERS = buffers
x   = the desired number of buffers - between 1 and 99

In order to allow certain applications to run well, a minimum number of buffers is necessary. The database program dBase IV instruction manual states that the program requires at least 15 buffers.

Example:
Increase the number of buffers for use with dBASE IV

Procedure: Write the following instruction in CON-FIG.SYS:

```
BUFFERS=15
```

Determining the maximum of files which can be run simultaneously. Information can only be written to a file or read from a file if the file has been opened. For each open file, the operating system manages a data structure (file control block, FCB), in which the status of the file is registered (open/closed). Normally, MS-DOS works with eight FCBs - a program can then read and write in a maximum of eight files. A larger number is required in the case of some programs. In previous DOS versions, each FCB occupied 39 bytes, from version 3.0 onwards, this is 48 bytes.

The FILES instruction determines the maximum number of files which can be open simultaneously.

Command: Change the amount of files which can be open simultaneously

```
FILES=x
```

FILES   = files
x   = maximum number of simultaneously open
          files - between 8 and 255 (prior to version
          3.0, between 1 and 99)

Example:
Increase the maximum number of open files to 20 with regard to usage of dBase IV.

Procedure: Write the following instruction in CON-
FIG.SYS:

```
FILES=20
```

Changing the program break mode. In chapter 1, we
mentioned that you can discontinue the running of the
operating system by using the key combinations Ctrl+C
or Ctrl+Break. The operating system will only accept
this command in the standard mode if it is reading or
writing data at that moment.
Thus, in the standard mode, it is not possible to break
off a program if it is not engaged in exchanging data
with the screen, the keyboard, the printer or via a com-
munication port.

**The BREAK instruction switches the break-off
mode of the operating system on and off**

Command: Break off a number of system functions

```
BREAK [ON/OFF]
```

BREAK = break, discontinue. This instruction on its
         own produces the current mode
ON   = extended break-off mode
OFF   = limited break-off mode (default value)

Example:
While starting, set the computer to the extended break-
off mode. Subsequently, examine the current break-off
mode.

Procedure: Type the following command in CON-
FIG.SYS:

```
BREAK=ON
```

Type the BREAK command behind the prompt when
the computer has been started up. The operating system registers 'BREAK is on'.

Adjusting the date and time format. Normally, the supplier will have applied the proper settings concerning the way in which the date and time are displayed, but if that has not happened, MS-DOS uses the American registration. This can be troublesome for the United Kingdom, due to the fact that the order of sequence of the days and months is the other way around. If you do not wish to conform to this standard, you will have to alter the CONFIG.SYS file to produce another method of display.

The COUNTRY command sets the date and time format.
Command: Adjust the date and time format

```
COUNTRY=x
```

COUNTRY = land
x   = country number. This is 044 for the
            United Kingdom. Specifying this acti-
            vates the customary way of registering
            the date and time, and also the unit of
            currency and the decimal point.

Other configuration commands

The SHELL instruction installs a different command interpreter than COMMAND.COM (or an extra command interpreter).

Command: Install a command interpreter

```
SHELL=[d:]file[.ext]
```

SHELL = shell, casing
d: = the drive where the new command in-
          terpreter is located

The LASTDRIVE instruction defines the maximum number of drives that the operating system may use.

Command: Specify a maximum number of drives

```
LASTDRIVE=1
```

LASTDRIVE   = last drive
l   = letter between A and Z

The value of LASTDRIVE may not be less than the number of drives present. If you have one diskdrive and a harddisk, that is minimally C.

7   Using the harddisk

Excepting DISKCOPY and DISKCOMP, all the commands which we have discussed up until now apply to both diskettes and harddisks. Where the applications differ, we have stated that fact explicitly. With the basic skills you have now acquired, you should be able to work with the harddisk.

When preparing a harddisk for optimal use, you should be familiar with several procedures which you have not yet dealt with using diskdrives:

■ Formatting the harddisk for the first time.
■ Creating a structure for the files.
■ Taking a number of safety measures.

Although, in daily use, instructions using the harddisk differ little or not at all from instructions using the diskdrive, the greater capacity makes it necessary to apply more regulations. Follow the advice which is given in various places in this book. If something should go wrong with the harddisk, a great deal of data could all be lost at once.

Make a copy on a diskette of the data on the harddisk (see section 7.3).
Be extremely careful when transporting the computer - the hardddisk is very sensitive to bumps (see section 7.4).
When you have switched off the computer, wait until you do not hear the harddisk rotating anymore before switching it on again.
When using the FDISK, FORMAT, RECOVER and DEL *.* instructions, data can be lost very easily. Be extremely careful with these instructions.

7.1 Preparing a harddisk for use

Partitioning the harddisk

When working with MS-DOS, you can divide the hard-disk into a maximum of four completely independent areas or partitions. This is useful if you wish to use different operating systems in your computer. Further study of this subject matter lies outside the scope of this book - most readers will only use MS-DOS with the harddisk.

You must make at least one partition for the MS-DOS operating system on the harddisk. To do this, an *external system program* is necessary. This is loaded in the computer memory from the system diskette in drive A:.

The FDISK instruction activates the program which partitions the harddisk.

Command: Partition the harddisk

```
FDISK
```

FDISK   = fixed disk

The program generates a menu. Confirm standard option 1 to create a DOS partition. The size of the harddisk and the MS-DOS version determine the appearance of the subsequent menus. In the most simple case of a medium-sized harddisk (20 Mb, for example), you may only respond Yes or No to the question as to whether you wish to use the entire harddisk for MS-DOS. If you answer Y, the program will ask you to place the system diskette in drive A: and to implement a warm start (reset). Subsequently, you only have to format the hard-disk in the same way as a diskette.

Example 52: Create one partition for MS-DOS on the harddisk

```
A:\>fdisk                                                        (1)

                        MS-DOS Version 5.00                       (2)
                      Fixed Disk Setup Program
               (C)Copyright Microsoft Corp. 1983 - 1991

                          FDISK Options

    Current fixed disk drive: 1

    Choose one of the following:

    1. Create DOS partition or Logical DOS Drive
    2. Set active partition
    3. Delete partition or Logical DOS Drive
    4. Display partition information
    5. Change current fixed disk drive


    Enter choice: [1]                                            (3)



    Press Esc to exit FDISK                                      (4)
```

```
              Create DOS Partition or Logical DOS Drive          (5)

    Current fixed disk drive: 1

    Choose one of the following:

    1. Create Primary DOS Partition
    2. Create Extended DOS Partition
    3. Create Logical DOS Drive(s) in the Extended DOS Partition



    Enter choice: [1]



    Press Esc to return to FDISK Options
```

(1) Drive A: is the current drive and the system diskette is located in this drive. Activate FDISK.
(2) The main menu of the program. The number of options depends on your configuration.
(3) The default option is [1]. In this example, you only have to confirm your choice by pressing Enter.
(4) Press Esc if you do not wish to use any of the avail-

able options. The program will then return to the prompt, A>.
(5) If you have chosen the first option, the menu will be replaced by this menu. Confirm the standard reply 1, because only one partition should be created. In the case of more extensive configurations, more choices are available in (2) and (5).

Formatting the harddisk and copying the system files

System

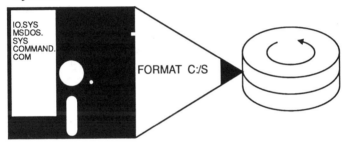

You do not need a system diskette if your computer has a harddisk containing the system programs.
In section 4.3 we saw how system files can be copied to a new diskette simultaneously with formatting. The procedure is the same in the case of the harddisk. Place the system diskette in drive A: and give the command:

```
A>FORMAT C:/S[/V]
```

The command formats the harddisk C: and then copies the system files from A: to C: using the /S option. If you also wish to allocate a name of maximum eleven characters to the harddisk, specify the /V option along with the command. At completion, the program will ask for a name for the disk.
Subsequently, copy all external system programs from the system diskette to the harddisk:

```
A>COPY *.* C:
```

From this moment onwards, the operating system will use the files on the harddisk when starting up if drive A: is not locked. It does not matter whether a diskette is located in this drive or not. The computer's internal starting procedure always looks for the system files in drive A: first. If the diskdrive is locked without system files being available, the system will state an error message: 'Non-System disk or disk error. Replace and strike any key when ready'. Open the drive and press any key.

SELECT, an abbreviated procedure for a system diskette

From MS-DOS version 3.0 onwards, you can have the operating system regulate a system diskette or the harddisk. In this case, the original system diskette, or a copy of it, is needed.

The SELECT instruction executes the following tasks:

■ Formats a new or used diskette/harddisk
■ Copies the system files (IO.SYS, MSDOS.SYS, COMMAND.COM).
■ Automatically writes the CONFIG.SYS configuration file with a COUNTRY instruction for the proper registration of date and time, the unit of currency and the order of sequence of sorting. This file is saved on the new disk.
■ Automatically writes the AUTOEXEC.BAT start-up file with the request for the specification of date and time, the statement of the MS-DOS version, a command for the path to the directory containing the DOS instructions and, if necessary, the keyboarddriver (KEYB) pertaining to a specific country. (The terms Path and Directory will be dealt with in section 7.2.) This file is also saved on the new disk.
■ Creates an apart directory for the external system programs if you specify this in the command.
■ The SELECT instruction copies the external system

programs to the specified directory. If this parameter
is not specified in the command, the external programs are placed in the root directory.

Take into account the following features of SELECT:

■ All information on the target diskette will be deleted.
  Accordingly, it is preferable to use this instruction for
  a new, unused diskette.
■ You can only specify A: or B: as source drive.
■ The target drive can be a diskdrive or the harddisk.
■ On the source diskette, all files should be located in
  the root directory, otherwise SELECT will not be able
  to find them.
■ If the target drive is a high-density drive (HD), you
  must also use a HD diskette. With respect to the total
  size of the files, you should not use a diskette which
  has a capacity of less than 720 Kb.

CAUTION: In SELECT, the format command deletes all
information on the target diskette. Especially if you wish
to apply this command to the harddisk, it is extremely
important to make a backup of all data.

The SELECT instruction activates an *external system
program* - ensure that the system diskette is located in
drive A: or drive B:.

**The SELECT instruction automatically creates a
disk containing a configuration file and a start-up
file.**

```
SELECT [[d1:] [d2:][path]] country code
keyboard code
```

SELECT   = choose
d1:   = the source drive A: or B:. The de-
                  fault drive is A:.
d2:   = the target drive: diskdrive or
                  harddisk. Normally, this is drive B:.
path   = the target directory for the exter-

nal system programs. The default directory is the root directory.

country code   = a number, corresponding to the international telephone network number (044 for the UK).

keyboard code   = two letters - UK for the United Kingdom.

From the 4.0 version onwards, the SELECT instruction works completely differently. Using a menu system, you make a selection from all possible setups. The result is similar to that of previous versions.

7.2   Managing files on the harddisk

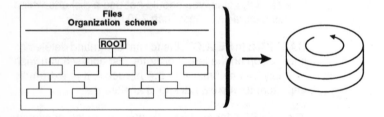

Using directories. A harddisk is a background memory with a large storage capacity, almost always 20 Mb or more. A 20 Mb harddisk can contain just as much information as 55 to 60 diskettes of 360 Kb.

It is a reasonable presumption that the average diskette contains around twenty files. Therefore on a harddisk, hundreds of files can be stored. Thus, it is not easy to always have a clear view of these. The list of files is awkwardly lengthy and it takes a couple of seconds before all the files can be displayed. In addition, there is a real danger that commands using wildcards can unintentionally delete or rewrite too many files.

From version 2.0 onwards, MS-DOS provides the possibility of organizing files in groups with their own names -

(sub)directories - on diskettes and harddisks. You are allowed to subdivide the structure of the groups as much as you wish. In the case of a 360 Kb diskette, that is really only worth the effort if there are more than 112 files on the disk. On a harddisk, a maximum of 512 files can be placed in the file list, without using directories. Directories have the following advantages:

■ orderly layout
■ quick access
■ the influence of the command does not extend further than the specified (or current) directory.

The normal directory of a disk is always the root directory. This is the main directory of the directory tree. In order to avoid referring to subsubsubdirectories eventually, we shall call all subdivisions 'directories' regardless of their level.

Each directory may be divided into many subdirectories. The operating system manages a directory in the same way as a file. Accordingly, the same rules apply to the names: eight characters and, if required, a point with an extension of three characters.

An example of the file structure of a harddisk is illustrated on the following page.

(1) The root directory contains all the system files.
(2) There are five directories whose names clearly express their contents: BASIC and Pascal represent the interpreter/compiler with their programs, all kinds of text files and the word-processor, and two standard applications: a calculation program with spreadsheets and a graphics program with images.
(3) The TEXT directory is subdivided into a directory for the program files for WordPerfect and two directories for other kinds of text - personal (LETTERS) and business (MEMO).
(4) The MEMO directory contains directories for three kinds of business texts: mailing, internal office announcements and meetings records.

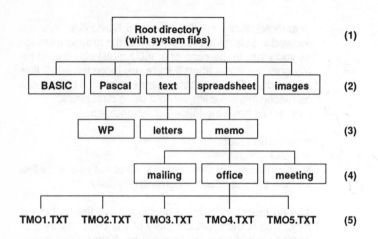

(5) The names of the internal announcements indicate the directory structure: TMO1.TXT (\Text\Memo\Office).

You can also save the external system programs from the root directory in a separate directory, \DOS for example.

Creating a directory

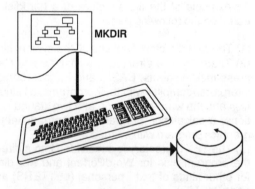

There is an *internal system program* for making a new directory - neither the system diskette nor the DOS directory from the harddisk is needed.

The MKDIR (or MD) instruction creates a directory under the current directory or under the root directory if you specify the entire path, beginning with the backslash \ of the root.

Command: Make a directory

```
MKDIR [d:][\]directory name[\directory name...]
MD [d:][\]directory name[\directory name...]
```

MKDIR	= make directory
MD	= abbreviated version of MKDIR
d:	= letter of the drive to which the command applies
\	= (backslash) the beginning of the path to the new directory. Without \ at the beginning, the command applies from out the current directory.
directory name	= name of a directory (analogous to a file name). Each subsequent name (preceded by \) indicates a lower level.

Example 53: Making the directories shown in the above scheme on the harddisk C:.

```
C:\>mkdir \basic                    (1)

C:\>md pascal                       (2)

C:\>md text                         (3)

C:\>cd text                         (4)
C:\>md memo

C:\>cd memo                         (5)
C:\>md office

C:\>md \text\memo\office            (6)
```

(1) Makes the BASIC directory in the root directory. Due to the backslash at the beginning, it does not make any

difference from which directory you give this instruction. See below, at the CD instruction, how to request the current directory. See section 8.2 how to include the current directory in the prompt.

(2) Assuming that the root directory is the current directory, the PASCAL directory is created in the root directory in this way.

(3) As in (2), but now for the TEXT directory.

(4) The first command makes the TEXT directory the current directory (see the outline below)). The second command creates a directory with the name MEMO in the TEXT directory.

(5) Switch to MEMO and make the OFFICE directory there.

(6) You could also have made the OFFICE directory without having to use the switch commands. (The TEXT and MEMO directories must already exist!)

Using files in (lower) directories

A directory structure is constructed in a way which makes it impossible to edit or delete files in more than one directory simultaneously. Accordingly, the DEL*.* command applies to the current directory alone. It is possible to copy files from one directory to another.

When the computer is started up, the root directory is normally the current directory. In order to be able to read or write in files in a directory, it is necessary to make the directory current. The switch command activates an *internal system program* - neither the system diskette nor the DOS directory from the harddisk is required.

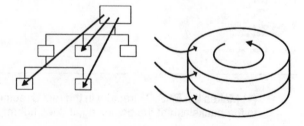

**The CHDIR instruction (or CD) switches to the speci-
fied directory. The Instruction on Its own produces
the current directory.**

Command: Activate a directory

```
CHDIR [d:][\]directory name[\directory name...]

CD [d:][\]directory name[\directory name...]
```

CHDIR	= change directory
CD	= abbreviated version of CHDIR. CD on its own produces the current directory.
d:	= letter of the drive containing the desired directory
\	= (backslash) the beginning of the path to the new directory. Without \ at the beginning, the command applies from out the current directory.
directory name	= name of the directory which is to become the current directory. A backslash (\) alone switches to the root directory.

Example 54: Switch to other directories and display the
current directory

```
C:\>chdir basic                    (1)

C:\>cd \text\memo\office           (2)

C:\>cd text                        (3)

C:\>cd memo                        (4)
                        -
C:\>cd office                      (5)


C:\>cd
C:\>text\memo\office               (6)

C:\>cd\                            (7)
C:\>cd                             (8)
C:\>
```

(1) The root directory is the current directory. The command switches to the BASIC directory.

(2) An abbreviated command to switch to the OFFICE directory.

(3),(4),(5) These three commands together produce the same result as the command in (2).

(6) CD on its own displays the current directory.

(7) Switch back to the root directory.

(8) Displays the current directory, the root directory.

Displaying the directory

The operating system does not automatically state that the switch to another directory has taken place successfully.

The PROMPT instruction enables you, among other things, to alter the appearance of the prompt so that the current directory is always displayed (see section 8.2). The 'PROMPT pg' command generates a prompt showing the current directory. You can give this command at any chosen moment, or include it in AUTOEXEC.BAT. Proceeding from the previous example, for instance:

```
C:\>TEXT\MEMO\OFFICE>
```


Displaying the contents of a directory

If you request the list of files using DIR alone, you are able to see by the first two lines of the list whether the current directory is the root directory or not.

In any directory, the first two lines contain the standard registration for the current directory (.), and the parent directory (..) (see example 57). Using the double period, you are able to switch immediately to the parent directory without having to enter the name. You may repeat the double period. In the directory structure in the example, by using the CD..\..\.. instruction, you switch from C:\TEXT\MEMO\OFFICE back to C:\.

The <DIR> code in the file size column means that the specified file is a directory.

Starting up a program located In a directory

In example 57, we shall attempt to start up the
GWBASIC BASIC interpreter in the root directory. This
cannot happen because the program is not located in
the current directory. We shall rectify this in the example
after the error message. The file list now displayed by
DIR shows that the proper directory has become current. Requesting GWBASIC will now be successful.

Example 55: Displaying a directory list of files and starting up a program

```
C:\>cd\                                          (1)

C:\>gubasic                                      (2)
Bad command or file name

C:\>cd basic                                     (3)

C:\BASIC>dir                                     (4)

 Volume in drive C has no label
 Volume Serial Number is 184A-546C
 Directory of C:\BASIC

 .            <DIR>       17/09/92    10:11       (5)
 ..           <DIR>       17/09/92    10:11       (6)
 WINFORM      <DIR>       17/09/92    10:12       (7)
 GUBASIC  EXE    80592 24/07/87     0:00          (8)
 INTER    BAS    46225 09/04/91     5:00
 OUBBLES  BAS    24103 09/04/91     5:00
         6 file(s)      150920 bytes              (9)
                       7913472 bytes free

C:\BASIC>gubasic                                 (10)
```

(1) Switch to the root directory.
(2) Attempt to start up the GWBASIC interpreter. This
produces an error message because the program is not
located in the current directory.
(3) Switch to the BASIC directory.
(4) Request the file list of the current directory.
(5) The period shows that the current directory is not the
root directory.
(6) The double period is the registration for the parent
directory.
(7) The directory WINFORM is located under the current directory.

(8) The BASIC interpreter is located in the current directory.

(9) The operating system treats all directories as if they were files - this means a total of six in the BASIC directory.

(10) It is now possible to start up the GWBASIC interpreter from out the BASIC directory.

In the description of the instructions in all previous examples, only *d:* has been specified to represent the drive. To keep matters simple, we have made the root directory on the diskette or harddisk the point of departure for all instructions up until now.

It is also possible to execute commands in a directory other than the current one, if you specify the names of the programs and files using the path from the current directory to the required directory (or, to be sure, the complete path from the root directory,\).

The backslash \ (in the sense of 'root directory') serves as a reference point for the operating system when looking for names of files and directories. This sign is a component of a search string, which is a hierarchical sequence of directory names, separated by backslashes. A series of directory names like this is mostly called a *path*.

If the path begins with a backslash, the operating system begins searching from out the root directory (the highest level). Without that sign, the system begins searching from out the current directory.

If you wish to use a file in another directory than the current one, it is necessary to specify the path to the file, in front of the file name.

In order to start up a program located in another directory, specify the path, a backslash and the name of the program, in that order of sequence.

Summary

Programs and data files can be copied and activated (loaded and started) if you specify the correct path for both source and destination file.

If you start up a program outside the current directory, it has no automatic relationship to the data files which belong to it. In this case, you should specify the entire path (see example 56).

Example 56: Using program files and data files in various directories on the harddisk (see the directory structure mentioned above).

```
C:\>cd text                                  (1)

C:\>up                                       (2)

memo\office\tmo1.txt                         (3)

C:\text\up>                                  (4)

\text\memo\office\tmo1.txt                   (5)

C:\>copy \text\memo\office\tmo1.txt \        (6)

C:\>copy \basic\prog.bas text                (7)

C:\>\basic\gubasic                           (8)

SAVE"\basic\prog.bas"                        (9)
```

(1) Switch to the TEXT directory.
(2) Start up the WordPerfect word-processor from out the TEXT directory.
(3) We wish to change the TMO1.TXT file in the OFFICE directory. Load this file in WordPerfect from out the directory in which you have started up WordPerfect (TEXT). Do this using the Shift-F10 key combination and type the required path. It is not necessary to specify the entire path from the root directory (TEXT\MEMO\OF-FICE\TMO1.TXT) - from out the current (TEXT) directory is sufficient. MEMO and OFFICE are located under this. (The diagram does not display the WordPerfect screen.)

(4) Using this instruction, the word-processor is started up beginning at the root directory. The word-processor now has no direct access to files in the TEXT directory.

(5) Loads the same file as in (3). In this case, it is necessary to specify the path from out the root directory.

(6) Copies the TMO1.TXT file to the root directory. It is not necessary to type the first backslash if the root directory is current. In the example shown, the instruction is independent of the current directory.

(7) The PROG.BAS program which has been saved in ASCII format in the BASIC directory is to be copied to the \TEXT directory (pay attention to the necessary backslash here).

It is possible to edit the BASIC program listing using a word-processor if you have saved the program within GWBASIC in ASCII format using the ",A" option.

(8) Start up the BASIC interpreter GWBASIC, which is located in the BASIC directory, from out the root directory. (The diagram does not show the GWBASIC screen.)

(9) From out GWBASIC, the PROG.BAS program is saved in the BASIC directory using the BASIC command, SAVE (the root directory is current).

Switching made easier with a batch file

If the harddisk is managed using a directory structure, you must either continuously switch to other directories or repeatedly type (long) paths.

Using a batch file, you can quickly switch directories and immediately start up a program if required. Save batch files like these under an obvious name in the root directory, so that the operating system can always find them.

Example 57: Create a TX.BAT batch in the root directory which switches to the TEXT directory and activates the WordPerfect word-processor.

```
C:\>cd \                        (1)

C:\>copy con tx.bat             (2)
cd \text                        (3)
up                              (4)
^Z                              (5)
    1 file(s) copied

C:\>_

C:\>tx                          (6)

cd \text                        (7)
\text\up                        (8)
```

(1) Switch to the root directory.
(2) Make the TX.BAT batch file using the COPY CON command.
(3) Switch to the TEXT directory.
(4) Activate the WordPerfect word-processor from the TEXT directory.
(5) Conclude the batch file and save it (in the root directory).
(6) Activate the batch file.
(7) and (8) Batch file ECHOs.

Activating executable files from out a random directory

The operating system can only directly execute files with the .COM, .EXE, and .BAT extensions (without having to make use of an interpreter). When a program like this is activated, the operating system searches in the current directory or in the directory specified in the path instruction.

MS-DOS has an instruction which saves you having to type the paths to the executable files. This instruction stores one or more paths to the directories containing the executable files in a separate part of memory, the environment memory. These paths remain active as long as the computer is on, or until you delete the paths.

When the instruction for permanent paths has been given, the operating system searches first in the current directory, and then in the directories which are specified in the path instruction. The instruction activates an *internal system program* - neither the system diskette nor the DOS directory on the harddisk is needed.

The PATH instruction installs permanent paths to the specified directories. PATH alone shows the active paths.

Command: Install paths

```
PATH [[d:]path[;[d:]path]...]
```

PATH   = path. The instruction on its own displays the current paths.

d: = letter of the drive for which the path is valid

path   = description using \ and directory names

You can also activate an executable file which is not in a permanent path if you activate the file by using a batch file located in the BATCH directory. This BATCH directory must be located in the permanent path.

Example 58: Installing paths

(1) The BASIC directory, containing the BASICPRO directory for the programs, is located in the root directory of the harddisk. The command shown makes the BASICPRO directory current.
(2) The instruction creates two paths which are always accessible from out the root directory (they both begin with a backslash). These are the paths to the BASIC directory and, separated by a semi-colon, to the root directory \ itself.

```
C:\>cd basic\basicpro              (1)

C:\>path \basic;\                  (2)

C:\>path                           (3)
PATH=\BASIC;\

C:\>diskcopy a: b:                 (4)

Insert SOURCE diskette in drive A:

Insert TARGET diskette in drive B:

Press any key to continue . . .
^C

C:\>cd \                           (5)

C:\>path \text                     (6)
```

(3) The instruction on its own requests the current paths. The display of these is on the following line.

(4) To test this, from out the BASICPRO directory, we shall activate the DISKCOPY program which is located in the root directory. The process is successful, and we discontinue this immediately using Ctrl+C.

(5) Switch back to the root directory.

(6) Install a path to the \TEXT directory containing the WordPerfect word-processor.

Caution: A PATH instruction gives the PATH environment variable a new value! The previous value will be lost and you will no longer have access to the BASIC directory from out a random directory.

Activating non-executable files from out a random directory

From MS-DOS version 3.3 onwards, it is possible to establish paths not only to executable files (programs), but also to (passive) data files and text files. Many programs cannot load corresponding data files from out a directory other than their own. The PATH instruction is unable to provide a solution here.

If you activate the word-processor from out the Word-Perfect directory, and subsequently wish to edit a chosen text in another directory, that can only be done if you specify the path in front of the name of the text file (as seen from out the WordPerfect directory). We have already seen an example of this in points (3) and (5) in example 56.

From version 3.3 onwards, there is an *external system program* available enabling you to install a path which is also valid for non-executable files. The *first time* that you activate this command, the system diskette or the DOS directory from the harddisk is needed.

From MS-DOS version 3.3 onwards, you can install, activate and delete paths using the APPEND instruction

Command: Install paths to general files

```
APPEND [/e][/x][;][[d:][path];[d:][path];...]
```

APPEND   = append. The instruction on its own activates the current search path.

/e   = environment. This instruction saves the path in an environment variable. You can activate the variable using the SET command.

/x   = executable. Makes the path valid for executable files.
Note:
The /e and /x options may not be defined simultaneously with a path. In this case, two instructions are necessary (see example 61).
APPEND /E /X plus 'APPEND path' is equivalent to 'PATH path'. Both types of paths may be installed simultaneously.

;   = 'APPEND ;'installs the NIL path - it deletes the current search path.

d: = the drive for which the path is valid.

path   = \ plus directory name. The total length of the path (separated by ;) has a maximum of 128 characters.

Example 59: Install two paths to general files, activate
them, test them and delete them again

```
C:\>append /e /x                        (1)

C:\>append \wp\letters;\wp\ccc          (2)

C:\>append                              (3)
APPEND=\WP\LETTERS;\WP\CCC

C:\>cd \                                (4)

C:\>type test.txt                       (5)

This is a test

C:\>append ;                            (6)

C:\>append
No Append                               (7)

C:\>
```

(1) Initially, the instruction has to be given without paths
(without the options, if necessary). The /E option saves
the path in a DOS environment variable so that you can
activate it using the SET instruction. The /X option also
validates the paths for executable files (.COM, .EXE,
.BAT).
(2) Installs two permanent paths to the (text) files in the
\WP\LETTERS and \WP\CCC directories. Pay attention
to the separation character, the semi-colon.
(3) The instruction on its own activates the current
paths. The operating system automatically changes the
small letters to capitals and places the equals sign between the variable and the current value.
(4) Switches to the root directory.
(5) The TEST.TXT file is located in the \WP\LETTERS
directory. The path enables you to display this file using
a command from out the root directory.
(6) Deletes the entire path which has been installed
using APPEND. The command has no influence upon
the value of PATH.
(7) The statement shows that there is no further path.

Displaying the directory structure (tree) of a diskette or the harddisk

The instruction activates an *external system program* which shows the directory tree on the screen. The system diskette or the DOS directory on the harddisk is needed.

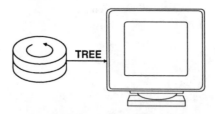

The TREE instruction produces a view of all directories, paths and file names on the harddisk or diskette. The Ctrl+PrintScreen key combination also transports the information to the printer.

Command: Display directory tree

```
TREE [d:][/F]
```

TREE   = tree. Displays the entire directory structure of the disk. Discontinue the display using Ctrl+NumLock or the Pause key. Continue by pressing a random key.
d: = drive to which the command applies
/F   = the program shows the file names also

Example 60: Displaying the harddisk tree, with and without files

(1) Requests the directory structure.
(2) Displays the first directory. The directory is not divided in subdirectories.
(3) The display is discontinued using Ctrl+C.
(4) Requests the tree and files.

```
C:\>tree                           (1)
Directory PATH listing
C:.
└──GEORGE                          (2)
^C                                 (3)

C:\>tree /f                        (4)
Directory PATH listing
C:.
    AUTOEXEC.BAT                   (5)
    CONFIG.SYS
    COMMAND.COM

    ──GEORGE
         ONE
^C

C:\>
```

(5) The /F option produces a list of files according to directory. The display is discontinued using Ctrl+C.

Deleting a directory

A directory can only be deleted if it is empty. The following points are important when using the delete command:

■ First delete all files using DEL*.* once you have made the directory current. (Request the list of files first, just to be sure.)
■ A directory can only be deleted from out a parent directory.
■ The root directory cannot be deleted.

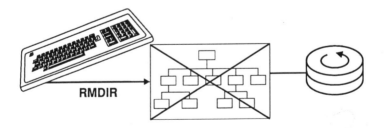

RMDIR

The instruction activates an *internal system program* -
neither the system diskette nor the DOS directory on
the harddisk is needed.

**The RMDIR (or RD) deletes an empty directory from
out the parent directory.**

Command: Delete a directory

```
RMDIR [d:]path
RD [d:]path
```

RMDIR   = remove directory
RD   = abbreviated version of RMDIR
d: = drive to which the delete command
               applies
path   = \ plus directory names. The last name
               is the directory to be deleted

Example 61: Delete directory

```
C:\>cd basic\basicpro                          (1)

C:\BASIC\BASICPRO>dir                           (2)

 Volume in drive C has no label
 Volume Serial Number is 184A-546C
 Directory of C:\BASIC\BASICPRO

.            <DIR>      17/09/92    10:35
...          <DIR>      17/09/92    10:35
INTER    BAS      41 17/09/92    10:49
        3 file(s)         41 bytes
                    7909376 bytes free

C:\BASIC\BASICPRO>del *.*                       (3)
All files in directory will be deleted!
Are you sure (Y/N)?y

C:\BASIC\BASICPRO>cd..                           (4)

C:\BASIC>rmdir basicpro                          (5)

C:\BASIC>cd basicpro                             (6)
Invalid directory
```

(1) Switches to the BASICPRO directory which we created in a previous example.

(2) Requests the list of files in the current directory. In addition to the two standard registrations concerning the directory, there is only the INTER.BAS program file.

(3) Deletes all files - in this case, only INTER.BAS.

(4) Switches to the parent directory (BASIC).

(5) Deletes the BASICPRO directory.

(6) Attempt to switch to the directory which has just been deleted. This is unsuccessful and causes an error message.

Example 62: Reorganizing the harddisk and activating the word-processor automatically

In this example, we shall integrate the know-how gained in the previous sections:

- dividing the harddisk effectively
- using directories
- using batch files.

The organizational structure of the harddisk is most orderly when the root directory contains only files which must be stored there (up to and including DOS version 3.3). These are the files:

- the program file of the command processor COMMAND.COM
- the configuration file CONFIG.SYS
- the start-up file AUTOEXEC.BAT.

(From version 4.0 onwards COMMAND.COM may also be located in another directory.)

In order to create an efficient organization, it is advisable to group files together in directories according to their functions: DOS files, applications, text etc. This has the advantage that all sorts of procedures concerning files (COPY, DEL) remain limited to the file category in question.

In the example, we shall create a DOS directory for the system programs (external commands), using the command:

```
C>MD \DOS
```

Subsequently, copy all programs from the external commands to this directory.

Important: If you do not know whether a file should belong to the \DOS directory or not, it is extremely important to make a backup of *all* files in the root directory in a reserve directory (\SAFE). Use the commands 'C>MD\SAFE' and 'C>COPY*.*\SAFE'.

If you are confident of what should be done, give the command:

```
C>COPY *.* \DOS
```

(You can, of course, copy wrong files to another directory later and/or delete superfluous files.) If you use the (copy of the) original system diskette, the following command will ensure that all the necessary files will be placed in the DOS directory:

```
C>COPY A:*.* \DOS
```

Subsequently, delete all the system programs from the root directory. Do *not* do this using the general file pattern *.* because other kinds of files are also stored there. Delete the files one by one (C>DEL DISK-COPY.COM etc.).

In the same way, create a particular directory for each application and copy the files to these: \WP, \DBASE, \LOTUS, etc. After all these manoeuvres, the root directory contains only directories. In the example, in addition to the\DOS directory, we have filled only \WP with corresponding files.

The system works most efficiently (quickest) if it can

find the system files in the root directory when starting
up. Therefore, copy these three files from the DOS directory back to the root directory. (Begin this task in the
root directory.)

```
C>COPY \DOS\COMMAND.COM
C>COPY \DOS\CONFIG.SYS
C>COPY \DOS\AUTOEXEC.BAT
```

In the example, the root directory appears approximate-
ly as follows:

```
C:\>dir                                        (1)

  Volume in drive C has no label
  Directory of C:\

DOS           <DIR>     17/09/92   10:56        (2)
WP            <DIR>     17/09/92   10:56
CONFIG   SYS       490 15/09/92   14:48
AUTOEXEC BAT       507 14/09/92   19:30
COMMAND  COM     47845 09/04/91    5:00
         5 file(s)       48842 bytes
                        276480 bytes free

C:\>dir \dos                                   (3)

  Volume in drive C has no label
  Directory of C:\DOS

.             <DIR>     17/09/92   10:56
..            <DIR>     17/09/92   10:56
ANSI     SYS      9029 09/04/91    5:00
^C
```

(1) Displays the list of files in the root directory.
(2) The \DOS and \WP directories and the three essential system files.
(3) Checks the list of files of the \DOS directory, discontinued by pressing Ctrl+C.

The CONFIG.SYS file is read and interpreted before
AUTOEXEC.BAT when the computer is started up. The
path is not yet installed (see chapters 1 and 6). This
means that the instructions in CONFIG.SYS to activate
programs and drivers must be equipped with the path
because these programs are no longer located in the
root directory.
Therefore, the command which activates the screen/-

keyboard driver in CONFIG.SYS must be changed from
DEVICE=ANSI.SYS to:

```
DEVICE=C:\DOS\ANSI.SYS
```

In the same way, the command concerning the specific
formats for date, time and unit of currency (from version
3.3 onwards) is:

```
COUNTRY=044,850,C:\DOS\COUNTRY.SYS
```

Using TYPE, examine whether these instructions
should be altered in your CONFIG.SYS. If necessary,
write a new version using the copy command 'COPY
CON CONFIG.SYS' or change the old version using
your word-processor (see section 6.2).
Only include the COUNTRY instruction in CON-
FIG.SYS if you have the 3.3 version (or more recent).

Subsequently, extend the path in AUTOEXEC.BAT with
the directories \DOS and \WP. This enables you to activate the external system programs and the word-processor later from out a random directory. Here also, you
may choose between writing the file once more using
'COPY CON AUTOEXEC.BAT' or changing the previous version using a word-processor. The path instruction is then as follows:

```
PATH=C:\DOS;C:\WP
```

Conforming to the scheme at the beginning of this section, two directories should be created for text files:
LETTERS and MEMO. Create these directories using
the commands:

```
C>MD \WP\LETTERS
C>MD \WP\MEMO
```

If you have followed the examples, the following structure of directories and files is now present on the harddisk:

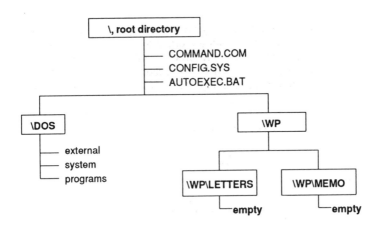

In principle, the contents of directories are not accessible from out another directory. The PATH instruction enables you to activate executable files (programs) in a directory which is not current. The APPEND instruction enables you to do the same with other files in a non-current directory.

What are the benefits of working like this?
If no path is specified, a file is automatically saved in the current directory, even if the program which creates the file is located in another directory. Accordingly, letters and memos are saved in the correct directory if you make that directory current at proper time. It is then very easy to make a backup of a category of files on a diskette in drive A by using just one command: COPY *.* A:.

In the example with which we are dealing at the moment (62), we shall make the \WP\LETTERS directory current using a batch file, and we shall activate the Word-Perfect word-processor from there. Thus, the letters which you then write will be saved in the \WP\LETTERS directory. When you quit the word-processor, the operating system will continue with the batch file - switch to the root directory and clear the screen.
We shall create an analogous batch file for writing memos.

As an aid to memory for activating batch files, we shall write a text file with a menu screen. This menu will appear on the screen when your computer is started up as a result of a TYPE instruction in AUTOEXEC.BAT. Write the menu using COPY CON or a word-processor.

```
+--------------------------------------------------+
| +----------------------------------------------+ |
| |            W O R D - P R O C E S S I N G      | |
| |            ------------------------------     | |
| |                                               | |
| |                  L = letters                  | |
| |                  M = memos                    | |
| |                                               | |
| |                                               | |
| |                                               | |
| |       Choose a letter and press Enter         | |
| +----------------------------------------------+ |
+--------------------------------------------------+
```

Save the text in the root directory under the name MENU.TXT. (Ensure that the word-processor saves the text without the formatting codes, in ASCII format.) You can extend the menu later with other options, according to your own requirements.

The DOS command, TYPE MENU.TXT shows the menu on the screen at any chosen moment. It is best if you clear the screen beforehand using the command CLS. Add these commands to AUTOEXEC.BAT.

Caution: To prevent batch file commands being displayed on the screen, specify ECHO OFF as the first instruction.

The last diagram in this section shows the contents of the new version of the AUTOEXEC.BAT file.

Each specified letter activates its own batch file: L.BAT and M.BAT. These batch files differ only in the directory which they make current.

It depends on your further computer pursuits whether it is more useful to include the \WP directory in the permanent path in AUTOEXEC.BAT, or to activate it using a new PATH instruction made with a batch file. The first method is more advantageous if you normally only use the word-processor. The second method saves time for the operating system, since it does not have to look for \WP if you wish to use dBase. These methods are illustrated in the example.

Due to the fact that the batch files differ so little, the best way to deal with them is to write, copy and alter them using a word-processor. This becomes more applicable the more you extend the menu.

The batch files contain the following instructions:

■ eliminate the display of instructions
■ switch to the work directory
■ make a path to the directory containing the word-processor
■ start up the word-processor
■ switch back to the root directory
■ clear screen
■ display menu.

In the diagram, the text from one of the batch files (L.BAT) is displayed.

```
C:\>type autoexec.bat              (1)

echo off                           (2)
path=c:\dos;c:\wp                  (3)
prompt $p$g                        (4)
keyb uk 850 \dos\keyboard.sys      (5)
cls                                (6)
type menu.txt                      (7)


C:\>type l.bat                     (8)

echo off
cd \wp\letters                     (9)
path=c:\wp;c:\dos                  (10)
wp                                 (11)
cd\                                (12)
cls                                (13)
type menu.txt                      (14)
```

(1) Displays the contents of AUTOEXEC.BAT on the screen.
(2) Eliminates the display of commands on the screen.

(3) Installs the path to the directories.

(4) Shows the current directory in the prompt.

(5) (In MS-DOS 3.3) Switches to the UK settings and the standard (USA) character set.

(6) Clears screen.

(7) Writes the menu on the screen.

(8) Displays the contents of the L.BAT batch file on the screen.

(9) Makes the directory \WP\LETTERS current. (In the case of the M.BAT batch file, this is the \WP\MEMO directory.)

(10) Installs a new path. You will notice that the priorities of the directories have been switched.

(11) Starts up the WordPerfect word-processor.

(12) Switches to the root directory after the word-processor.

(13) Clears screen.

(14) Writes the menu on the screen.

7.3 Protecting information on a harddisk

At various places in this book, we have emphasized that it is very important to safeguard information by keeping copies if it. You can use diskettes, a harddisk or cassette tapes (with a *tape streamer*) as storage media.

The same instructions apply to both diskettes and harddisks when making backups - thus, for brevity, we shall refer to diskettes alone. Due to the fact that special hardware and a non-standard driver are necessary to save information on magnetic tape, we shall not deal with this possibility here.

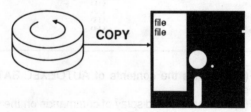

Safeguarding information by copying

The simplest method of safeguarding information is to copy it to a diskette. This applies not only to files containing information but also to programs. Some manufacturers have saved their programs in such a way that they can only be copied back to the harddisk using a special program. In cases like these, it is of no use to make a copy on a diskette of the version on the harddisk.

The COPY command can be used for files in one directory on the harddisk. Using COPY, you can copy one file, a group of files or all files from a directory.

Example 63: Copying individual files, groups of files or all files from a directory to a diskette in drive A:

```
C:\>cd \text\memo\office           (1)

C:\>copy tmo1.txt a:               (2)

C:\>copy x.txt a:                  (3)

C:\>copy x.x a:                    (4)

C:\>cd \                           (5)

C:\>copy \text\memo\office\tmo1.txt a:   (6)

C:\>copy \text\memo\office\x.x a:        (7)
```

(1) Switches to the OFFICE directory.
(2) Copies the TMO1.TXT file from the current directory to the diskette in drive A:.
(3) Copies all files with the .TXT extension to the diskette in drive A:.
(4) The same as (3), but now for all files.
(5) Switches to the root directory.
(6) Copies the TMO.TXT file from a non-current directory to the diskette in drive A:. The operating system requires the path to the file.
(7) Copies all files in the non-current OFFICE directory to the diskette in drive A:.

Copying a directory, including the files in the subdi-rectories

From MS-DOS 3.2 onwards, there is a new, extended copy command which not only copies individual files, groups of files and all files in a directory, but also copies entire directories, *including* the subdirectories. In addition, this instruction can copy to a diskette of a different format. This is impossible using DISKCOPY due to the dissimilar format, and using COPY, it can only take place in various stages. The extended instruction enables you to copy complete branches of the harddisk directory tree to diskettes, using one command.

The instruction activates an *external system program* - the system diskette, or the DOS directory on the harddisk or a path to it, will be needed.

The XCOPY instruction copies one or more complete directories, including the files in the subdirectories, from a harddisk or a diskette to another drive or another directory.

Command: Copy the directory structure

```
XCOPY [d:]path/d:[path] [d:][path]
    [/A][/D:date][/E][/M][/P][/S][/V][/W]
```

XCOPY	= copy directory, including files
[d:]path or d:[path]	= source directory or source drive. Specify at least one source directory [d:]path or source drive d:[path], otherwise the command will produce an error message. The options between the square brackets are not compulsory. *Path* represents the complete path from out the root directory.
[d:][path]	= if you do not specify a destination drive and a destination directory,

the directories or the files will be copied to the current directory (from where you activated XCOPY).

[/A]   = using this option, the command will only copy those files which have the *archive attribute*. The /A option does not alter the attributes of a file.

Explanation: The archive attribute is one of the codes which is registered on the diskette along with the file name. Files may have more attributes, but this topic lies outside the scope of this book. This attribute is assigned to a new file and to a file which has been altered.
You can make the status of an attribute visible using the command:

```
ATTRIB [d:path]file name
```

If the operating system replies with the letter A, the archive attribute of the file has been switched on.
You can switch this attribute on and off yourself by using the commands 'ATTRIB -A file name' or 'ATTRIB +A file name', respectively.

If the Read Only attribute has been switched on, the file cannot be altered (ATTRIB +R file name). Remove this blockage by specifying 'ATTRIB -R file name'.

[/D:date]   = the instruction copies only files which have been created since a given date.
Type the date according to the format you specified using the COUNTRY instruction in CONFIG.SYS. For the United Kingdom, that is dd-mm-yy.

[/E]   = empty. Using this option, you copy also the empty directories (without files). This option must always be accompanied by the /S option.

[/M]   = modify. The option has the same effect as /A, only, in addition, the archive attributes of the source files are deleted. The results in the files only being copied, using the XCOPY instruction (with /A or /M), if they have been altered in the meantime.

[/P] = prompt. Using this option, the instruction asks for each file whether it should be copied or not. Respond with y/Y or n/N.

[/S] = sub. Copies one or more directories, including the subdirectories. The empty directories are only copied if you have also specified the /E option.

[/V] = verify. Using this option, the instruction checks if there are differences between the originals and the copies.

[/W] = wait. The command is only implemented after pressing a random key. This allows you the chance of placing an empty diskette in the destination drive, which is handy if you include the command in a batch file. You can cancel the command using Ctrl+C.

Example 64: Copy the TEXT directory, as shown in the diagram, with the subdirectories LETTERS and MEMO, from the harddisk to a diskette in drive A: and then from the diskette in drive A to a diskette in drive B:.

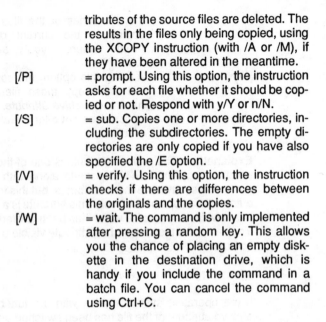

```
C:\>xcopy \text a:\text /s /e          (1)
Does TEXT specify a file name          (2)
or directory name on the target
(F = file, D = directory)?d
Reading source file(s)...              (3)
\TEXT\LETTERS\L1.TXT
\TEXT\LETTERS\L2.TXT
\TEXT\MEMO\MEMO1.TXT
\TEXT\MEMO\MEMO2.TXT
        4 File(s) copied

C:\>dir a:                             (4)

 Volume in drive A has no label
 Directory of A:\

TEXT        <DIR>      17/09/92   11:23
        1 file(s)          0 bytes
                      354304 bytes free

C:\>xcopy \text\ a:\text\ /s /e        (5)

C:\>xcopy a: b: /s /e                  (6)
```

(1) Copy the TEXT directory plus the TEXT\LETTERS
and TEXT\MEMO directories from the harddisk C: to
the diskette in drive A: under the same name, TEXT.
The /S option copies all subdirectories from the specified directory. The /E option copies the empty directories in TEXT. The last option is superfluous since files
are located in both directories. There is no fixed order of
sequence for the options.

(2) The program cannot deduce from the command
whether the target is a directory or a file. If another
backslash is located behind the target, TEXT, it can
only be a directory. Then there is no prompt. (see point
(5).)

(3) The program states that it is reading the source files
and gives a list of the copied files, including their path.

(4) Due to the fact that there is not enough room in the
diagram to show the contents of the diskette in drive A:,
we shall only display the file list in the root directory,
without the headlines (we presume that the diskette
was originally empty).

(5) The same command as in (1). The backslash behind
the objective ensures that TEXT can only be interpreted
as being a directory. The program does not have to ask
for more information.

(6) Copies the \TEXT directory with all its directories
and files from the diskette in drive A: to the diskette in

drive B:. In this case, it is not necessary to specify the source directory, because no misunderstanding is possible. The same applies to the destination - if the diskette in drive B: is empty, there is no doubt as to where the directories and files should be saved.

Protecting data using a special program

It is rather laborious to make a complete copy of the harddisk using the standard copy instruction. You have to specify each directory separately in order to copy its files. In addition, you only copy the files using this method and not the tree structure of the directories.

(Copying back is particularly tedious - first you have to reconstruct the tree and then work out which file on the diskette belongs to which directory on the harddisk.)

Another disadvantage is inherent in the copying process itself - the operating system gives an error message if a file on the harddisk does not fit on the target diskette. It would be an exceptional coincidence if the end of the file fitted exactly into the available space on the diskette.

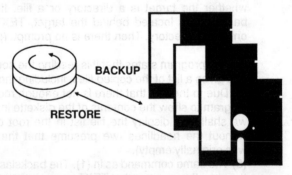

MS-DOS provides a program which can deal with all the problems mentioned above. Using this program enables you to:

- make a backup of all files and directories
- write all data from the backup(s) back to the harddisk
- make a backup of a part of the files
- make a backup of only those files which have been saved (altered) after a specified date.

The program states when the diskette is full. It will then ask for another diskette and will subsequently continue copying.

The destination diskette must already be formatted. Without the /A option, the files which are already located on the diskette will be deleted.
Write successive numbers on the diskette labels.
The contents of the backup diskettes can only be written back in the same order of sequence as written to the diskettes.

The safeguard procedure requires two *external system programs* - one to make a copy of the information and one to write the copy back to the harddisk. Thus, the system diskette, the DOS directory of the harddisk or the path to it is needed. Both instructions accept wildcards in the file names.

The BACKUP instruction activates a program which makes a backup on diskette of information on the harddisk (or vice versa).

Command: Make a copy of information on the harddisk

```
BACKUP [d1:][path][file.ext]
d2:[/S][/M][/A][/D:date]
```

BACKUP   = reserve copy
d1:   = source drive
file.ext   = name of a particular file of which you
              wish to have a copy
d2:   = target drive
/S   = subdirectories. Makes a backup of all
              files and directories.

/M	= makes only a backup of those files which have been altered since the previous backup instruction
/A	= append. Adds the backups to the files which are already located on the diskette.
/D:date	= makes a copy of only those files which have been saved (altered) since the specified date

Example 65: Making a backup of a harddisk on diskettes in drive A:.The copy program is located in the root directory on the harddisk.

```
C:\>backup c: a: /s                              (1)

Insert backup diskette 01 in drive A:            (2)

WARNING! Files in the target drive
A:\ root directory will be erased
Press any key to continue . . .

*** Backing up files to drive A: ***             (3)
Diskette Number: 01

\AUTOEXEC.BAT                                     (4)
\CONFIG.SYS
^C

C:\>backup c: a: /s/m                             (5)

C:\>backup c:\text\*.txt a:                       (6)

C:\>backup c: a:/s/d:88-10-92                     (7)

C:\>backup c:\basic\*.* a:/a                      (8)
```

(1) Drive C: is current. The command activates the copy program which is located in the root directory. C: is the source drive, A: is the target drive. The /S option makes a backup of all the harddisk files and directories.
(2) The system registration requests the first diskette to be placed in the target drive. Ensure that the (formatted) target diskettes contain no indispensable data. This will be deleted. The program states where the information is located on the diskette. In the example, there is only the root directory. The command is implemented after striking a random key.

(3) The program ascribes consecutive numbers to the diskettes.

(4) The program first copies the root directory with its files and then the directories successively with their contents. In the example, the command is discontinued by pressing Ctrl+C.

(5) Copies all those files from the harddisk which have been altered since the previous occasion a backup was made.

(6) Makes a backup on diskettes of all files with the extension .TXT in the TEXT directory of the harddisk.

(7) Makes a backup on diskettes of all files which have been altered since the 10th of August 1992.

(8) Copies all files from the BASIC directory from the harddisk to the diskette in drive A: and adds them to the files which are already located there.

The RESTORE instruction activates a program which writes the backup back to the harddisk from diskettes which have been copied using BACKUP

Command: Write data back to the harddisk

```
RESTORE d1: d2:[path][file.ext] [/S][/P][/M][/N]

            [/B:date][/A:date][/E:time][/L:time]
```

RESTORE = restore
d1:   = drive of the diskettes containing the backups (source drive)
d2:   = drive to which the backups are to be written (target drive)
path   = destination directory for the backups
/S   = subdirectories. All files and directories.
/P   =prompt. The program asks permission to copy files back if they have the Read Only attribute on the target drive (or are more recently dated there (see below)).

The following options are available from version 3.3 onwards, but not in all releases. Consult your DOS manual.

/M   = modified. Writes back only those files
                      which have been altered since the pre-
                      vious backup.

/N   = not. Writes back only those files which
                      are no longer located on the target drive.

[/B:date]   = before. Writes back only those files
                      which have been altered prior to the speci-
                      fied date.

[/A:date]   = after. Writes back only those files which
                      have been altered since the specified
                      date.

[/E:time]   = earlier. Writes back only those files
                      which have been altered before the speci-
                      fied time.

[/L:time]   = later. Writes back only those files which
                      have been altered after the specified time.

[/D]   = display. Displays files on the backup
                      disk which match specifications.

Example 66: Write the backup files and directories from
the diskette in drive A: back to the harddisk

```
C:\>restore a: c: /s                    (1)

Insert backup diskette 01 in drive A:   (2)
Press any key to continue . . .

*** Files were backed up 17/09/1992 ***  (3)

*** Restoring files from drive A: ***
Diskette: 01
\AUTOEXEC.BAT
\CONFIG.SYS
^C

C:\>restore a: c:\text\*.txt            (4)

C:\>restore a: c:\basic /s              (5)
```

(1) Writes all files and directories, which were copied to
the diskette in drive A: using BACKUP, back to the root
directory of the harddisk.

(2) The program requests the first backup diskette to be
placed in drive A:. Proceed by pressing any key.

(3) The program has registered that the correct diskette
is in the drive and copies the files and the directories

successively. The instruction is discontinued by pressing Ctrl+C.

(4) Copies all files with the extension .TXT from A: to the C:\TEXT directory.

(5) Copies all files and directories on the diskette in drive A: to the C:\BASIC directory. (This directory must already exist on the harddisk.)

7.4   Protecting the harddisk during transport

A harddisk is very sensitive to jolts. If a harddisk is not protected during transport, the write/read head can easily damage the magnetic layer of the disk. Not only can data be lost, the mechanism which moves the head can be deregulated, resulting in an inability of the operating system to find information.

Therefore, before you transport a computer with a harddisk, take the following measures:

- make a backup of all data (see section 7.3)
- place the read/write head in a safe position.

To carry out this second safety measure, there are utility programs which turn the read/write head to a safe position. Consult the documentation about your computer to find the name of this program - common names are SHIPDISK, XPARK and PARK.

Some manufacturers supply the parking program on the diagnosis diskette in the manual. Place the diskette in drive A: and restart the computer. The diagnosis program will be activated and a menu will be displayed. Select the parking option.

Recent computers, particularly the laptops, automatically place the heads in a safe position as soon as you switch off the power. Consult the manual to find out if your computer also does this.

8   Other instructions

8.1   Interface settings for screen, printer and communication

The MS-DOS operating system contains an instruction which influences various interfaces and peripheral devices:

- the screen (colour graphics adapter)
- printer (parallel interface)
- communications port (serial interface).

The screen: number of characters per line

It is occasionally useful if the screen is able to display larger characters - for example, if you wish text to be read by a group of people. The screen has several modes: 80 or 40 characters per line, colour or black-and-white, and monochrome (only 80 characters).

The MODE instruction specifies the screen mode.

Command: Specify the screen mode

```
MODE n [,M[,T]]
```

MODE   = mode
n   = number of characters, (colour) mode

- 40 or 80: the current (colour) mode remains active
- BW40 or BW80: black-and-white display
- CO40 or CO80: colour display
- MONO: switch to monochrome adapter (only 80 characters per line)

M   = move. Moves the contents of the screen one
         (40 characters) position or two positions - to the
         left if you specify L for M or to the right if you
         specify R.
T   = test. This instruction places a test pattern on
         the first line.

**The printer: specifying the number of characters
per line and the space between the lines**

**The MODE LPT instruction regulates the number of
positions per line and the number of lines per inch
used by the printer.**

Command: Specify the print width and line spacing

```
MODE LPT#: [n][,[m][,P]]
```

MODE LPT = printer mode (line printer)
= number of the parallel printer port (1, 2
           or 3). Instead of LTP1 you may also write
           PRN.
n   = number of characters per line (80, 132)
m   = line spacing (6 or 8 lines per inch, lpi)
P   = permanent. Up to and including version
           3.3, this option ensures that the operating
           system keeps on trying to send characters
           to the printer if it is not yet ready.

From version 4.0 onwards, the repeat option can have
four values:
■ E (error, the default value) produces the error code
  from a port which is in use
■ B or P states 'busy' to the operating system if an error
  occurs
■ R states 'ready' to the operating system if an error occurs
■ N (none) means taking no action.

Specifying the communications port

You can connect a serial printer, modem, mouse or acoustic device to the communications port (*serial interface, RS 232C port*) of your computer.
You can only use a peripheral device with a serial connection if you regulate the computer interface to the values specified by the manufacturer of the device. For a *serial printer*, you have to specify the following instructions. (Mostly, the printer is connected to the parallel port.)

The detour version of the MODE instruction transports the output to the printer via the communications port.

Command: Connecting the printer to the serial interface

```
MODE LPT#[:]=COMn[:]
```

MODE LPT = printer mode
#[:]   = number of the printer (1, 2 or 3)
COMn[:]   = serial interface (COM1 or COM2)

The MODE COM instruction regulates the communications port for serial (asynchronic) transmission.

Command: Regulate the serial interface

```
MODE COMn[:]baud[,[parity],[data bits],
[stop bits][,P]]
```

MODE   = regulating the mode
COMn[:]   = serial interface (COM1 or COM2)
baud   = transmission speed (bits per second).
            You only need to specify the first two digits
            of the following valid numbers: 110, 150,
            300, 600, 1200, 2400, 4800, 9600, 19200.

parity   = each character if checked to ensure proper transmission. The valid values are: N (none, no parity bit), O (odd, uneven parity), E (even, even parity). The default value is E.

data bits   = the number of bits sent per character (7 or 8, the default value is 7)

stop bits   = the end criterion (1, 1.5 or 2 bits - the default value is 2 in the case of 110 baud, otherwise 1)

P   = same as the option in the MODE LPT instruction. (There is also a difference in the versions before and after 3.3.)

Example 67: Alterations in the specifications dealing with the screen, the printer and the communications port. Drive A: is the current drive - load the external system program from out the root directory of the harddisk.

```
A:\>c: mode 40              (1)

A:\>c: mode 80,r,t          (2)

A:\>c: mode lpt1:132,8      (3)

A:\>c: mode lpt1:=com1      (4)

A:\>c: mode com1:12,n,8,1,p (5)
```

(1) The screen mode becomes 40 characters per line, without the colour mode changing.
(2) The screen mode becomes 80 characters per line, without the colour mode changing. In addition, the screen contents shift two positions to the right and a test pattern appears on the first line.
(3) The printer works with 132 characters per line and 8 lines per inch.
(4) Output to the printer is sent via the communications port COM1.
(5) The communications port is installed for a serial printer with 1200 baud, without parity control, 8 data

bits, 1 stop bit and without the routine which tests time-out errors.

8.2   Altering the prompt

The appearance of the system prompt differs according to the supplier. The standard form has the drive letter with a 'greater than' sign. You can make the prompt more informative by adding, for example, the date, time, current directory, a chosen text etc. Using so-called 'escape' functions, you can accentuate (parts of) the prompt, have them blink etc.

If you specify the instruction dealt with here, without parameters, the prompt will regain the standard form. The instruction activates an *internal system program* - the system diskette, the DOS directory on the harddisk or a path are not needed.

The PROMPT instruction changes the form of the system prompt.

Command: Change the prompt

```
PROMPT $x [$x] . . .
```

PROMPT   = prompt. Without parameters, the opera-
          ting system will continue using the stand-
          ard prompt.

$ = dollar sign, the beginning code of a para-
          meter. Without the dollar sign, the charac-
          ters will be shown literally as text.

x   = a character from the following list:
          d =   date
          t =   time
          p =   current directory of the current
                   drive
          n =   current drive
          v =   version of MS-DOS
          g =   >, 'greater than' symbol
          l =   <, 'smaller than' symbol

b =	|, pipe symbol
q =	=, equals sign
h =	back one space and delete previous symbol
e =	escape sign
_ =	two symbols - CR plus LF (cursor to beginning of next line)

Examples:

```
C>PROMPT $d $t$g
```

Result: Tue 04/08/92 15:56:26.32>

```
C>PROMPT $p$g
```

Result: C:\>

```
C\>PROMPT
```

Result: C> (standard system prompt)

8.3　Assigning drive commands

The configuration with which you are working will not always have the same settings as those an application might expect. This can be problematic if the application expects a drive which your computer does not have. In a case like this, it is possible to allocate another letter to a certain drive. The instruction activates an *external system program* - the system diskette, the DOS directory on the harddisk or the path to this, is needed.

The ASSIGN instruction registers a drive under another letter.

Command: Assign another name to a drive

```
ASSIGN x=y
```

ASSIGN   = allocate
x   = original drive letter
y   = new drive letter

Example:

```
C>ASSIGN C=B
```

9   Basic concepts

9.1   The working of the operating system

The processor is the heart of the computer. This is a collection of complex electronic switches which repeat simple calculations and logical processes at high speed, in such a way that they are able to solve a problem by well-organized co-operation. The variation in problems which the processor must be able to solve is so large that it is not possible to include a suitable problem-solving method, in terms of an electronic component in the computer, for all cases. The system would be much too extensive and thus too expensive. In addition, it is not possible to make improvements to a solution method which is established in a chip. This could only be done by replacing chips or relocating them internally.

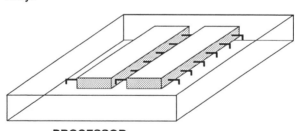

PROCESSOR

A chip consists of a collection of electronic equivalents of reasonably easy standard calculations and other processes. The accounts and the organization of the processes needed to solve a problem are written in applications. The standard calculations in these changeable programs are executed by *operating programs* or *system programs* which, in turn, regulate the elementary steps carried out by the electronics in the processor. The collection of system programs which run the working of the computer is called the *operating system* or, in short, the system. (Mostly one uses the word 'system' in the broader sense, to include the hardware.)

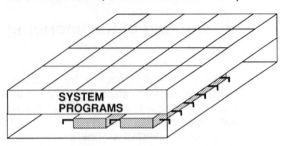

It is obvious that it is easier to distribute diskettes with an improved and more extensive version of the system programs than to supply all computers with a new set of processor chips. Computer programmers who are occupied with programs for the internal organization of computers are called system programmers.

Programs and information are entered using the keyboard or a scanner (previously also using punch cards and tape). If these have previously been entered in a way legible to the computer, they can also be read from an external storage medium, such as a harddisk or cassette tape etc.
Programs are mostly started up from the keyboard by entering their name. The processor and the operating system interpret the instructions in the program and implement them.

Information and the contents and results of programs can be displayed on a monitor (screen), using a printer or a graphic plotter in the form of letters and numbers, as a picture, or in the form of an acoustic or optical signal.

Programs and original information need not be entered every time they are to be used if they have already been saved on a storage medium (diskette, cassette tape, harddisk). This makes it easier to exchange information and results.

The tasks of the operating system

The operating system consists of a collection of programs. These programs, of course, can only be executed when they have been loaded into computer
memory. For this reason, they are loaded automatically
into memory when the computer is started up, mostly
from the harddisk, sometimes from diskette.

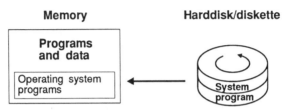

Memory   **Harddisk/diskette**

The operating system programs are loaded into a part
of the memory, which is, thus, no longer available for
applications. The very first loading instructions could not
be carried out by the computer if only programs on disk
were available. To implement these instructions, the
computer language codes are permanently stored in a
chip. The starting-up codes are located in the *bootstrap
loader*. This program implements the *boot load* (loading
operating system process). Other elementary routines
are located in the BIOS chip (basic input output system).

In the permanent memory, the computer is only able to
read (read only memory, ROM). This contrasts with the
random access memory (RAM) which is used for both
reading and writing.
There are also microcomputers which have their entire
operating system in ROM. This does not have to be
loaded from an external storage medium, but the system has to make a copy of the work memory. This takes
place much more quickly than reading from a disk.
Some operating systems only load the most-used system programs in the work memory (the internal instructions), other instructions are only loaded when they are
activated (external instructions).

As soon as the most important operating system programs have been loaded, they take charge of the operating processes in the computer. The diagram shows, by means of arrows, the influence exerted by the operating system.

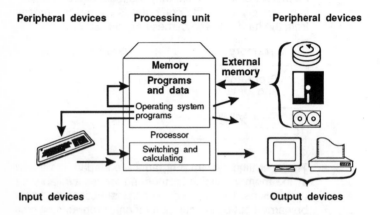

Some programs are constantly needed by the computer - they form the so-called *kernel* (IO.SYS, MSDOS.SYS) of the internal management. These procedures can be divided into three groups of routines with different functions:

- executing user commands (job control)
- implementing a program: starting up, implementing measures, discontinuing, quitting, dealing with errors, management of virtual memory (storing parts of memory on harddisk), managing multitasking, managing multiple usage, etc. (task control)
- managing the transport of data between system unit, the storage media and other peripheral devices (data control). Errors which occur in this process are also registered here.

Utility programs also play an important part, but they do not have to remain constantly in memory.

■ External instructions often execute recurring standard duties: copying, sorting, data transport, testing hardware and software.

MS-DOS compared to other operating systems

The demands on an operating system are mainly dependent on the capacity and speed of the hardware. The capabilities of a computer always depend upon the combination of the hardware and the operating system. When assessing the capabilities of a computer system, one should take into account:

■ calculation speed
■ storage capacity and writing and loading speed
■ availability of virtual memory
■ availability of multi-user possibilities
■ availability of multitasking possibilities.

In the light of these features, computers are divided into four categories according to size: mainframes, minicomputers, personal computers and home computers. The first two categories generally differ only in processing speed and memory capacity. In the latter two categories, also called microcomputers, there is seldom talk of configuration in a multi-user environment or of a system which works with multitasking. However, the most recent types of personal computers, ATs, tend more and more towards the minicomputer in terms of features.

The MS-DOS operating system has been developed for personal computers (PC, XT, AT). Up until version 3.0, MS-DOS was only usable in a single-user environment. Multitasking and virtual memory management has only become possible with the OS/2 operating system which is distant family of MS-DOS.
It is possible to use MS-DOS in a system from a higher size category if that computer works with a set of instructions which emulates the DOS instructions.

The Digital Research predecessor, CP/M 86, is no longer a rival to MS-DOS. It is not yet certain just what the succesor to MS-DOS will be. This may be OS/2, a completely new version of MS-DOS, or it may be the universal multi-user UNIX system from AT&T. IBM and Siemens have introduced comparable systems on the market, under the names XENIX and SINIX, respectively.

9.2   MS-DOS structure and working

As mentioned in the first chapter, the letters MS, in the name MS-DOS, are an abbreviation of the name of the manufacturer, Microsoft. The letters DOS represent 'disk operating system'. The magnetic storage disk may be a harddisk, which is also called a fixed disk, or a floppy disk (diskette). We shall now only refer to diskettes, but the information also refers to operations using the harddisk. (Chapter 7 deals specifically with harddisks.)

The MS-DOS operating system was developed for the Intel microprocessors 8088 and 8086 Intel, but it is also compatible with the more powerful successors, 80186, 80286, 80386 and 80486 from the same firm.

MS-DOS is also usable on computers with processors from other manufacturers if the specific hardware routines are emulated by extra system programs.

The MS-DOS operating system is generally supplied on a diskette along with the computer. The computer starting-up routine loads the most important system programs. Subsequently, these take charge of the management for implementing instructions and programs. This way of working is time-consuming, but it has the advantage that the operating system can be easily replaced by an improved version (see section 9.1). In this section, we have already seen that the operating system consists of two kinds of system programs - internal and external. The internal system programs IO.SYS and MSDOS.SYS cannot be found on the system disk-ette using the DIR command. They have the *hidden* file attribute. They are registered when the CHKDSK com-mand is executed (see section 4.6). The third essential system program is the *command interpreter* COM-MAND.COM. This program is visible in the normal list of files.

The three essential programs remain in memory as long as the computer is switched on - they are *resident*. Nevertheless, there is a difference, within the modules of COMMAND.COM, between 'essential' and 'import-ant'. Components in the latter category may be re-placed in memory, if necessary, by other programs. If you quit a program which has overwritten parts of COM-MAND.COM and return to the operating system, you will receive a request to place the system diskette in the current drive. The operating system can then reload the missing parts:

```
Place diskette with COMMAND.COM in drive x:
```

If you do not wish to give commands using external in-structions, you can remove the system diskette from the diskdrive and insert a diskette with an application.

Instructions on the system diskette

The COMMAND.COM program examines all input when the computer has been started up and compares the command text to an internal list of reference words. If a word coincides with a word on the list, the corre-sponding module in COMMAND.COM is activated and carried out immediately. Instructions which belong to the resident part of the operating system are called *in-ternal instructions*. These instructions are readily ac-cessible because they are already located in memory - they only have to be activated.

In the case of a reference word which does not occur on the internal list, the instruction may refer to an external

DOS command or to an application. COMMAND.COM
searches in the directory of the current drive for a program containing the specified name. If it is located
there, the program is loaded into memory and activated.
The advantage of system programs which are only
loaded when they are explicitly named is that a large extent of memory remains available for applications.
These system programs are called *external instructions*. Thus, you can only use them when the MS-DOS
system diskette is placed in the current diskdrive. (Unless the files are located on a harddisk and you have installed a path to them.)

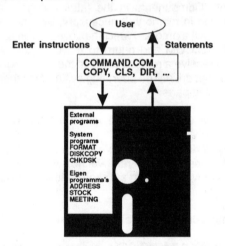

If COMMAND.COM cannot find the instruction name in
a directory on the system diskette, this means that the
requested program is unavailable (or the name has
been specified erroneously). The command interpreter
then states:

```
Bad command or file name
```

Change an erroneous command by entering it once
more, correctly. If necessary, replace the current diskette with a diskette containing the desired program. Accordingly, it is important to inexperienced users that an

application explicitly states when another diskette is required. For this reason, we have clearly stated, when
dealing with commands in previous chapters, whether
they were internal or external commands.

MS-DOS and computer type

The fact that two computers have the same processor
does not mean that they react in exactly the same way
to the MS-DOS operating system. There are differences
according to manufacturer, particularly in the interfaces
between the hardware and the main MS-DOS system
programs. The manufacturers qualify their goods using
two differing descriptions:

■ compatible with MS-DOS
■ completely (100%) compatible with the IBM PC or
   with the industry norm.

The first claim merely means that methods of instruction
specification and the results of the system programs are
similar.
The second claim means that the applications which
have been developed for the IBM PC will work in the
machine in question, without any problem. It remains to
be proved whether this is true or not for all applications
which you may acquire.

Even without MS-DOS, personal computers already
contain a limited operating system. The *basic input output system* (BIOS) consists of routines which manage
the input and output at the most fundamental level
(thus, 'basic'). The BIOS forms the link between the
hardware and the IO.SYS input and output program of
the operating system. (This must be absolutely the first
program on the system diskette.) The BIOS and IO.SYS
together load the remaining main system programs in
memory from the starting-up disk.

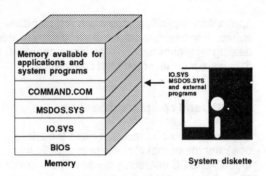

Memory   **System diskette**

If the BIOS of a compatible computer is not identical to that of an IBM PC, this must be compensated by IO.SYS. For a long time, small differences were necessary in order to allow clones to circumnavigate the IBM copyrights. This entails that the complete operating system of one computer is not automatically usable on another. The IO.SYS program straightens this out so that the two other main system programs are interchangeable (unless the manufacturer has altered something here too).

9.3   Input devices

Under the MS-DOS operating system, personal computers are mostly operated in conjunction with the keyboard. In the configuration, there are additional mains switches and specific switches on the devices: brightness and contrast on the monitor, line length and font on the printer etc.

During the last couple of years, the *mouse* has become more popular. If you shift this operating device over the table, a rubber ball underneath rolls along two small wheels which measure the distance moved. These measurements are translated into movements of the *cursor* on the screen. This shows the current working position. The shape of the cursor (block, arrow) differs according to the program. Using this, you can select an object or an option in a list (menu). By pressing one of the buttons on the mouse, you can give the instruction to execute the corresponding task: marking, deleting, drawing etc. The mouse was previously a device which was particularly used in graphic programs. Nowadays, the mouse is being increasingly used as a indication device in a menu system, replacing typed instructions via the keyboard. A driver must be installed for the mouse on the computer. This is supplied along with the mouse.

The *joystick* is available to operate computer games. This input device works in roughly the same way as the mouse. The movements of the joystick produce guide signals which relocate the movable object in the game. The buttons cause actions which differ according to the game.

Keyboard

Most manufacturers of compatible computers make use of the keyboard layout which was designed by IBM, although this is not absolutely necessary in terms of hardware.
Since 1983 IBM has brought three types of keyboard on to the market: PC, AT02 and AT03 (advanced technology). (The abbreviation AT, with the same meaning, is now also used for the most recent type of personal computers.) The AT03 type is also called the MF (multifunctional) keyboard. Due to the fact that the AT02 type was only in supply for a short time, most clone manufacturers have adopted the PC and MF keyboards as standard.
PC keyboards are now only supplied with PCs and XTs. Personal computers of the XT technology type are PCs which are suitable for a harddisk. Nowadays, MF keyboards are widespread with all types of personal computers.

Keyboard compatibility. It is not possible to just replace one kind of keyboard with another. In principle, each type of keyboard requires its own driver, but there are also MF keyboards nowadays which have a switch

enabling you to change from the PC/XT mode to the AT
mode.

Keyboard and character set. Normally, keyboards
generate the American character set. This is troublesome for languages with tildes, accents and other special signs (French, German, for example). Keyboards
for these countries often deviate in terms of layout and
have other lettering on the keys. Using an appropriate
keyboard driver, you can link a suitable character set to
your keyboard (see chapter 7 concerning the DEVICE
instruction for CONFIG.SYS). In addition, the keyboard
driver adjusts the registration of the date and time to the
national standard.

9.4   Types of diskette

In compatible personal computers, four types of diskette
are now in use, each having its own specific demands
on the diskdrives, according to size and/or write-den-
sity.

From MS-DOS 2.0 onwards:
a) 5.25 inch diskettes with double density (DD, 360 Kb).

From MS-DOS 3.0 onwards:
b) 5.25 inch diskettes with high density (HD, 1.2 Mb).

From MS-DOS 3.2 onwards:
c) 3.5 inch diskettes with double density (DD, 720 Kb).

From MS-DOS 3.3 onwards:
d) 3.5 inch diskettes with high density (HD, 1.44 Mb).

Type A, the standard diskette for PCs and XTs
Personal computers with the 8088 or 8086 processor
have, as a rule, at least one diskdrive. Mostly, they have
a second diskdrive or, in the case of an XT, a harddisk.
Diskettes with the following features should be placed in
the diskdrives:

5.25 inch	diameter of the diskette
double-sided (DS or 2)	information written on both sides
double density (DD)	information written in double density form
48 tpi	48 tracks per inch

MS-DOS formats this diskette in the following way:

- 40 tracks on each side
- each track is divided into nine sectors
- each sector has a capacity of 512 bytes (characters).

This means that the capacity of this diskette is 2x40x9x512=368,640 bytes. That is 360 Kb (1024 bytes is one Kb).

Some older types of diskdrive are only able to write on one side of the diskette. These drives can format one side for 180 Kb. To do this you must give the FORMAT command with the /1 option.
In the oldest versions of MS-DOS (1.0 and 1.1) diskettes were formatted with eight instead of nine sectors. Diskettes like these can be formatted using more recent versions of FORMAT if you specify the /8 option. Single-sided capacity is 160 Kb, double-sided is 320 Kb.

Type B, the standard diskette for ATs. The more recent personal computers with the 80286 or the 80386 processor use diskettes with greater information density. ATs (advanced technology) use diskettes with the following features:

5.25 inch	diameter of the diskette
double-sided (DS or 2)	information written on both sides
high density (HD)	information written with high density
96 tpi	96 tracks per inch

If no options are specified, from version 3.0 onwards, FORMAT will format these diskettes in the following way:

■ 80 tracks on each side
■ each track divided into fifteen sectors
■ each sector has capacity of 512 bytes (characters).

This means that the capacity of this diskette is
2x80x15x512 = 1,228,800 bytes. This is 1.2 Mb (1 Mb =
1024 Kb = 1024x1024 bytes).

Caution: HD diskettes which have been formatted for
high density cannot be read by diskdrives for normal
density (DD). The other way around is generally possible
- a 1.2 Mb diskdrive is almost always able to read 360 Kb
diskettes.

In most 1.2 Mb diskdrives it is possible to format DD
diskettes if you use the FORMAT command with either
the /4 option or the combined option /T:40 /N:9 (see
section 4.3). These diskettes have, of course, a capacity of 360 Kb. On your own computer, a diskette which
has been formatted in such a way will cause no problems, but if you use it to exchange information on some-
one else's computer, there is a chance that reading errors may occur. Especially on other PCs and XTs, there
is the chance that the diskette will (appear to) be il-
legible. This is due to the fact that the method of writing
is different when using an AT than when using PCs and
XTs. In addition, the writing and reading heads may differ a little with respect to their positioning.
Practice shows that many of these faults can be
avoided if the diskettes are formatted in the diskdrive
which has to read them later.

Never format a DD diskette in a HD diskdrive without
using the options mentioned above.
Depending upon the diskdrive and the quality of the diskettes, it is sometimes possible to format a capacity
greater than 360 Kb, but these diskettes cannot be used
on another computer because they are not legible there.

Type C, the small diskettes for personal computers
From version 3.2 onwards, MS-DOS can work with 3.5
inch diskettes for personal computers. These diskettes

can be used along with 5.25 inch diskettes, or instead of
them. 3.5 inch diskettes are not only smaller and therefore handier in portable computers (laptops), they also
are protected by a much more sturdy plastic casing.
These diskettes have the following features:

3.5 inch	diameter of the diskette
double-sided (DS or 2)	information written on two sides
double-density (DD)	information written with double density
	(most manufacturers do not specify this)
135 tpi	135 tracks per inch

If no options are specified, FORMAT will format these
diskettes in the following way:

■ 80 tracks on each side
■ each track divided into nine sectors
■ each sector has capacity of 512 bytes (characters).

This means that the capacity of this diskette is
2x80x9x512 = 737,280 bytes. That is 720 Kb.

Caution: 3.5 inch diskettes cannot be used in a 5.25
inch diskdrive.

Type D, the small diskettes with high write density
From version 3.3 onwards, MS-DOS also uses 3.5 inch
diskettes with high write density. These diskettes have
the following features:

3.5 inch	diameter of the diskette
double-sided (DS or 2)	information written on both sides
High density (HD)	information written with high density
135 tpi	135 tracks per inch

If no options are specified, FORMAT will format these
diskettes in the following way:

■ 80 tracks on each side
■ each track divided into eighteen sectors
■ each sector has a capacity of 512 bytes (characters).

This means that this diskette has a capacity of
2x80x18x512 = 1,474,560 bytes. That is 1.44 Mb.

In most 1.44 Mb diskdrives, it is possible to format normal DD diskettes if you give the FORMAT instruction
with the combined option /T:40 /N:9. These diskettes
have, of course, a capacity of 720 Kb. (The remarks
concerning the legibility of type B also apply here.)
If you attempt to format a DD diskette in a HD drive
without the options mentioned above, this may be successful. If you are fortunate, these diskettes will not
cause problems on your own computer, but there is a
large chance of encountering problems when using
them in other computers. Most diskdrives will not accept
the instruction because they do not recognize the type
of diskette by the square hole in the HD diskette casing
(opposite the write protection sleeve).

Caution: It is impossible to read or to write a HD diskette in a diskdrive for normal write density (DD).

Exchanging information via diskettes

Diskettes are a very handy means of transporting programs and information files from one computer to the
other. This can only take place, of course, if the diskettes used are compatible with the diskdrives in both computers. The way in which the information is stored on
the diskette depends upon the diskdrive and the storage
format which the operating system uses. In order to be
able to use diskettes which have been formatted under
MS-DOS to transport files, it is necessary that both
computers be constructed according to the industry
standard.
Whether the transported *programs* also work on the
second computer is another matter. The software compatibility of a computer depends on the hardware and

the permanent components of the operating system (see section 9.2).

Passive *data files* do not cause problems with computers which are not fully compatible, as long as they are saved in ASCII format (American Standard Code for Information Interchange).

Copying, copy protection, copy programs

In principle, it is possible to copy, alter and delete the operating system, other programs and data files to a formatted diskette using one of the DOS instructions.
Some software manufacturers protect the copyright on their applications by making copying more difficult by using a programming trick, a deviating storage format or a physical blockage on the diskette. Copying is then no longer possible using the standard MS-DOS instructions. In practice, a new copy protection is always decoded quite quickly, and an appropriate copy program appears on the market.
Of course, it remains a fact that illegal copying is a form of stealing. Copying for third parties is only allowed if you have received explicit permission for this.

Write protection

You can protect diskettes against unintentional overwriting by using a write protection. In the case of a 5.25 inch diskette, you can tape over the notch with an opaque sticker. In the case of a 3.5 inch diskette, you can open the little sleeve to activate the protection. A protected disk can be read, but nothing can be written to it.
If you attempt to write on a diskette with write protection, the operating system gives an error message:

```
Write protect error writing drive A
Abort, Retry, Fail? _
```

Place an unprotected diskette in the drive (or remove
the protection) and reply with R (Retry).

Make a habit of protecting diskettes containing important programs or data immediately after saving, by applying a sticker or by opening the protection sleeve.
Put away a diskette only after you have attached a label
indicating the most important files and the date of saving. Write the information on the label first and then attach it to the diskette in order to prevent the pressure of
writing damaging the diskette surface.

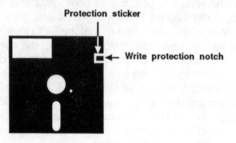

Protection sticker

←— **Write protection notch**

9.5   Types of file

A difference is made between a data file and a program
according to the nature of the information.

Data files are (orderly) collections of numeric, alphanumeric and graphic characters (ASCII codes 0 to 255
inclusive), which are stored in such a way that they can
be interpreted by an application.

Imagine you have written a letter using a word-processor
and you save it under the name INFO.TXT. The letters,
the punctuation marks and the numbers are located in
the INFO.TXT file. Using the word-processor, you can
transport the data to the screen or the printer later.

Other kinds of data files contain, for example, numbers
from a calculation program (spreadsheet) or picture elements (pixels) from an image.

```
Data file: INFO.TXT

----------------------------------------------------------------------

Dear Sir/Madam,


The Hieroglyph Company delights in being able to present a

demonstration of the new word-processing program "Chisel Up".


"Chisel Up" saves texts in the form of extensive ASCII codes on a

diskette. These files are legible on all compatible PCs.
```

Program files consist of a collection of instructions which are registered in two different ways:

Command file: If you write a program in the BASIC language which calculates interest, for example, you use instructions which you can read yourself. Instructions which people can read without expert knowledge are called program text or *source code*. This kind of file can be written, altered and saved using a word-processor in the same way as a text file. It is, in fact, literally a text file.

Object file: A computer cannot directly execute commands in the legible text form. First they have to be translated into much smaller instructions in a code which the processor can deal with. This is called machine code or *object code*. This information can also be saved in a file called an object file. A program which is available as an object file can be directly implemented by the computer (executable file).

Depending on the computer language, the translation program is called a *compiler* or an *assembler*.

There are translation programs which translate the commands in a command file one by one at the same time that the file is executed in memory - the machine code is temporary. Programs like these act as translators - that is why they are called *interpreters*. Examples are the 'traditional' BASIC interpreter and the dBASE III+ interpreter.

Program file	Program file
INTER.BAS	INTER.EXE
(program text)	(machine code)
-------------------------------------	-------------------------------------
10 INPUT K,P,D	1001110111011010
20 LET R=K*P*D/(100*360)	1110101010001001
	1010101111001111
30 PRINT R	1001000000101101

You can request and display the contents of a file using a DOS command or using a word-processor (see section 3.7). For most readers, the display is only legible if the file has been saved in ASCII format (text file and source code). Complicated and assembled files (object files) appear on the screen as a hotch-potch of strange signs. Files like these can only be decoded and made legible using special tools.

MS-DOS uses the following names for utility files when re-routing data, when linking program modules and when restoring damaged files:

```
%PIPE    NUL        FILEnnnn.CHK
@...     VM.TM = FILEnnnn.REC
```

The characters nnnn are increasing numbers from 0000 to 9999, inclusive.

The following names are reserved for the peripheral devices which MS-DOS has under its management:

```
AUX   COM1   CON   LPT1   PRN
      COM2         LPT2
                   LPT3
```

The extensions listed below are added by MS-DOS, by a translation program or by an application to a file name. In most cases, you are not able to influence this. You will encounter them reasonably often in the list of files on program diskettes.

.$$$	.BAS	.COM	.HEX	.MAP	.REL
.ASM	.BAT	.CRF	.LIB	.OBJ	.TMP
.BAK	.BIN	.EXE	.LST	.REF	

Grouping file names using a pattern

Normally, a separate command is required for each file which you wish to copy or delete. If you wish to copy four files, for instance, from diskette A to diskette B, four commands are necessary.

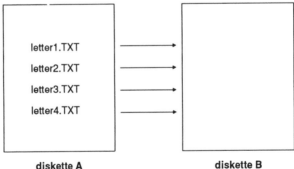

diskette A   **diskette B**

For situations like these, MS-DOS provides the possibility of combining commands using non-defined characters. These are called *wildcards*. A question mark represents any one character, an asterisk replaces characters at all subsequent positions starting at its own position.

The four copy instructions in the example can be condensed into one command:

```
COPY A:LETTER?.TXT B:
```

This command will also copy LETTER9.TXT although that may not be the intention. See also example 29 in section 4.4.

If you also wish to copy the backups to these letters (.BAK extension), you can replace the extension with an asterisk:

```
COPY A:LETTER?.* B:
COPY A:LETTER*.* B:
```

In the first column of the table, there are more examples of files which you can combine using a name including wildcards.

Files	File pattern
LETTER1A.TXT ... LETTER9A.TXT	LETTER?A.TXT
All BASIC programs	*.BAS
All files with the name EXAMPLE	EXAMPLE.*
All files	*.*

Appendix

A   Alphabetical list of MS-DOS instructions

Instruction	Result	Examples
A:, B:, C:	Change current drive	A>B: ->B> B>A: ->A> A>C: ->C>
APPEND (external)	Make path to data files	C>APPEND /E /X C>APPEND \WP\LET-TERS;\WP\MSDOS
ASSIGN (external)	Rename drive	A>ASSIGN C=B
ATTRIB (external)	Display/allocate file attributes	C>ATTRIB +RA LET-TER.TXT C>ATTRIB -RA LET-TER.TXT
BACKUP (external)	Make backup of data on harddisk	C>BACKUP C: A:/S C>BACKUP C:*.TXT A:
BREAK	Extend influence of Ctrl+C (also via CONFIG.SYS)	BREAK ON(OFF) (A>)BREAK
BUFFERS	Specify number of disk buffers; via CONFIG.SYS	BUFFERS=15
CALL	Activate batch file (.BAT) from out an-other batch file	CALL test CALL testmet 1 2 3 (Activate TESTMET.BAT with three parameters)

CHCP	Activate character set for specific country	A>CHCP 850 (standard character set)
CHDIR (CD)	Change current (sub)directory	C>CD text\letters C>CD basic
CHKDSK (external)	Check harddisk, diskette or files	A>CHKDSK B: A>CHKDSK B:*.*/V C>CHKDSK /F
CLS	Clear screen	A>CLS
COMMAND	Load extra command interpreter	A>COMMAND /C DIR C: A>COMMAND /E:400 /P
COMP (external)	Compare (copied) files	A>COMP A:tstfile1.txt B:tstfile2.txt A>COMP *.txt B:*.bak
COPY	Copy files	A>COPY A:NUMBERS.TAB B:NUMBERS.TAB A>COPY *.txt B: A>COPY data.* B: B>COPY *.* A: A>COPY A:letter1.txt+A:letter2.txt B:letters.txt
COPY CON	Make text file from keyboard (CONSOLE)	A>COPY CON part1.txt ... text ... ^Z
COUNTRY	Regulate country-oriented display; via CONFIG.SYS	A>COUNTRY=044,850,C:\DOS\COUNTRY.SYS (values for UK)
CTTY	Switch to other standard input/output device	A>CTTY COM1 (to serial interface) A>CTTY CON (back to CONSOLE)

DATE	Enter/request date	A>DATE (request, alter) A>DATE 12-08-92 (new date)
DEL	Delete files	A>DEL A:command.001 A>DEL B:storage.* A>DEL *.xyz A>DEL *.* (careful!)
DEBUG (external)	Test assembled pro- gram	A>DEBUG A>DEBUG test.com
DEVICE	Load driver; via CONFIG.SYS	DEVICE=ANSI.SYS
DIR	Display list of files	A>DIR A>DIR /P A>DIR /W A>DIR B:*.txt A>DIR B:command.*
DISKCOMP (external)	Compare copies of diskettes (made using DISKCOPY)	A>DISKCOMP A: B: A>DISKCOMP
DISKCOPY (external)	Copy entire diskette	A>DISKCOPY A: B: A>DISKCOPY B: A: B>DISKCOPY A: B:
DRIVPARM (existing drive) DRIVER (new logical drive)	Regulate device parameters for disk or tape drive; via CONFIG.SYS	DEVICE=DRIVPARM /D:2 /F:2 /H:2 /T:80 /S:18 (diskdrive 720 Kb)
ECHO	Switch display of commands on/off (for batch files), display statements (from batch file)	(A>)ECHO ON(OFF) (A>)ECHO statement

EDLIN (external)	Activate line editor	A>EDLIN test.txt A>EDLIN newfile.abc/B (binary load: ignore end-of-file)
ERASE	Delete file	(analogous to DEL)
EXE2BIN (external)	Convert .EXE file to .COM file	A>EXE2BIN command.exe command.com
EXIT	Quit Command interpreter (or SHELL)	C>EXIT
FASTOPEN (external)	Load a number of file directions for fast search	C>FASTOPEN C:=50 D:=34
FC (external)	Compare contents of two files	(analogous to COMP)
FCBS	Specify number of file control blocks; via CONFIG.SYS	FCBS=12,6 (opens a maximum of 12 FCBs simultaneously, the first six protected against automatic closure)
FDISK (external)	Partition harddisk	A>FDISK (presents a menu)
FILES	Specify maximum number of simulta-neously open files; via CONFIG.SYS	FILES=20
FIND (external)	Search for a string in a file (filter)	A>FIND "COMPUTER" B:letter.txt
FOR	Loop command (for batch files)	FOR %%x IN (t1.txt t2.txt t3.txt) DO TYPE %%x (display the contents of the three files success-ively)

FORMAT (external)	Prepare disk (be careful with hard-disks!)	A>FORMAT B: A>FORMAT B:/S A>FORMAT C:/V B>FORMAT A:/S/V
GOTO	Move command (for batch files)	GOTO end ... other commands ... :end
GRAFTABL (external)	Load extended character set (ASCII 128-255)	A>GRAFTABL 850 (standard character set)
GRAPHICS (external)	Enables display of graphic (colour) screen on printer	A>GRAPHICS
IF	Condition for the specified command	IF %==t1.txt GOTO display IF NOT EXIST t1.txt GOTO end
INSTALL (from MS-DOS 4.01 onwards)	Implement one or more of the resident programs FAST-OPEN, KEYB, NLSFUNC, SHARE in CONFIG.SYS (specify parameters if necessary)	C>INSTALL=C:\DOS\ FASTOPEN.EXE C:75
JOIN (external)	Addressing a drive as a directory	A>JOIN A: C:\TEST
KEYBxx (up to MS-DOS 3.2) KEYB (from MS-DOS 3.2 onwards) (external)	Load keyboard adjustment; via AUTO-EXEC.BAT	A>KEYBUK A>KEYB UK,850,C:\DOS\KEY-BOARD.SYS

LABEL (external)	Specify/alter name (max. 11 charac- ters) of a disk	A>LABEL B:TESTDISK
LASTDRIVE	Higher drive letter allowed (only mean- ingful in networks); via CONFIG.SYS	LASTDRIVE=M
MEM (external)	Display memory usage	A>MEM [/PRO- GRAM][/DEBUG]
MKDIR (MD) (external)	Make directory	C>MD \text\memo C>MD basic
MODE x (external) MODE LPT# (external)	Screen: number of characters per line Printer: specify char- acters per line, line spacing OR printer port	A>MODE 40 A>MODE 80,R,T A>MODE LPT1:132,8 A>MODE LPT1=COM1
MODE COMn (external)	Regulate serial inter- face	A>MODE COM1:12,N,8,P
MORE (external)	Display information per screen	A>TYPE t1.txt|MORE A>MORE<t1.txt A>TREE|MORE
NLSFUNC (external)	Select country- oriented data from a file	C>NLSFUNC [C:\DOS\COUNTRY.SYS] (or an own file)
PATH	Install paths for ex- ecutable files (.EXE, .COM, .BAT)	A>PATH \basic;\ A>PATH \text\memo
PAUSE	Discontinue display of batch file (unless ECHO is OFF, the prompt 'Press any key..' always appears)	PAUSE PAUSE statement

PRINT (external)	Print files using the print queue	A>PRINT t1.txt/P t2.txt A>PRINT com- mand.dat/C A>PRINT /T
PROMPT	Alter system prompt; redefine key from ASCII code X to Y	PROMPT $P $G PROMPT $e[X,Yp
RECOVER (external)	Reconstruct dam-aged files	A>RECOVER B:letter.txt A>RECOVER C:
REM	Place commentary in batch files and CONFIG.SYS	REM *** Commentary *** REM Remove diskette
RENAME (REN)	Rename file	A>REN B:old.123 B:new.456 A>REN t1.txt letter.txt
REPLACE (external)	Replace/supple-ment files on target disk from a source disk	C>REPLACE A:*.txt C:\WP\CCC /A
RESTORE (external)	Copy back backup copies (made using BACKUP)	A>RESTORE A: C:/S A>RESTORE A: C:*.txt
RMDIR (RD)	Remove directory	C>CD \text\memo C>DEL *.* C>CD \ C>RD \text\memo
SELECT (external)	Make new system diskette containing country-oriented data	C>SELECT A: B: 044 UK

SET	Display or initialize variables in the MS-DOS system environment	A>SET A>SET file=new.123
SHARE (external)	Allow simultaneous use of same file in network; reserve 4096 bytes for file information (AUTOEXEC.BAT)	SHARE /F:4096
SHELL	Install new command interpreter; via CONFIG.SYS	SHELL=C:\DOS\NEW-COMM.COM
SHIFT	Move batch file variables leftwards	Before: %4=t1.txt %5=t2.txt SHIFT After: %3=t1.txt %4=t2.txt
SORT (external)	Sort text file lines alphabetically	A>SORT <t1.txt >t2.txt A>SORT /R <a1 >a2 A>DIR|SORT >LPT1
STACKS	Define number and size (in bytes) of the stacks; via CONFIG.SYS	STACKS=0,0 STACKS=16,512
SUBST (external)	Address a path using a drive letter (/D means Cancel)	C>SUBST B: C:\WP C>SUBST B:/D
SYS (external)	Copy the MS-DOS system files later (to a formatted empty diskette)	A>SYS B:
TIME	Display/specify time	A>TIME A>TIME 12:32

TREE (external)	Display list of directories (/F also shows files)	C>TREE C: A>TREE C:/F
TYPE	Display contents of file on screen (on the printer using Ctrl+PrtSc)	A>TYPE table.dat A>TYPE C:\text\t1.txt
VER	Show MS-DOS version number	A>VER
VERIFY	Activate or request test mode for writing to disk	A>VERIFY (ON/OFF) A>VERIFY ... VERIFY is on/off
VOL	Show name of disk	A>VOL B: A>VOL
XCOPY (external)	Copy contents of directory, including subdirectories	C>XCOPY \text A:\text\ /E/S

Key combination	**Result**	**Remarks**
Alt+Ctrl+Del	Restart system (warm start)	Wait until harddisk has stopped!
Ctrl+PrtSc	Print screen contents; switch off function using same combination	Hardcopy
Ctrl+NumLock (Pause)	Stop screen roll	Continue by pressing any key

Index